BECOMING EMOTIONALLY FIT FOR THE GAME OF LIFE!

# PROCESS YOU TO SUCCESS

3 Steps to Reaching Higher Levels in your Life, Career, & Relationships

JEMIAH BATTLE

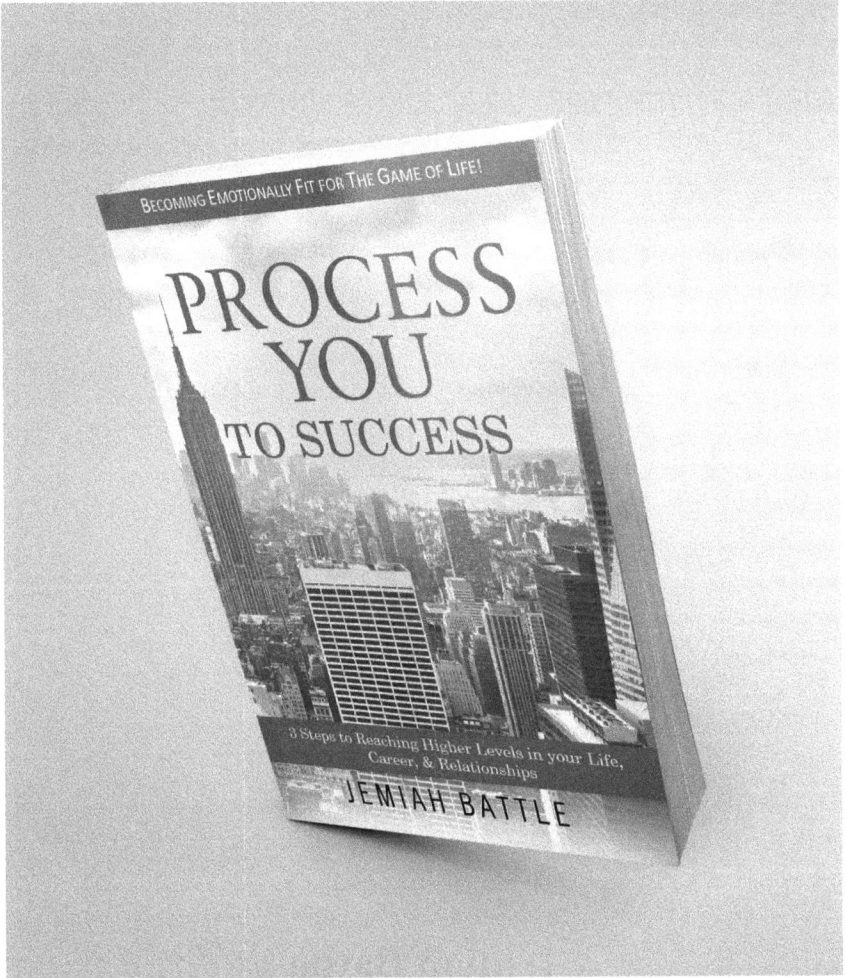

BY Jemiah Battle,CPC

# PROCESS YOU

## To

## Success

**Jemiah Battle**

PROCESS YOU to SUCCESS

Copyright 2015,2016 by JemiahBattle.com

Published by Renaj Publishing

Printed in the United States of America. For information and inquiries address Renaj Publishing, P.O. Box 24161, Greenville, S.C, 29616.

Cataloging-in-Publication data for this book is available from the library of Congress.

ISBN-13:978-0692646892

ISBN-10:0692646892

Renaj Publishing books are available at special discounts for bulk purchases in the U.S. by corporations, institutions, and other organizations. Please contact for more information.

This Book is dedicated to my wife Renea, my son Jaheim "Ja", and my daughter Amajinique "Maji", my mother Janie, my pops JB, my Pastor Wendell Jones, my spiritual mentor Dr. Radice Banks, Sheri Riley, T. Julian Gipson (Thanks for Believing in me when others didn't!), Bernell Ingram, CYMM, The Upstate Fatherhood Coalition, and the many others whose lives have motivated, encouraged, supported, and strengthened me in some way.

Thank You

# Table of Contents

# PROCESS YOU to SUCCESS

Jemiah Battle, is founder of The SELF Initiative, an Inspirational Speaker, and Certified Life coach & Success Architect specializing in EQ, relationship dynamics, Youth & Young Professional leadership development, Identity Development and social & life transitions. This book is based on the tested, results-focused strategies that he uses daily with private clients and in his own life and relationships. He believes in real world Solutions for real world people. Jemiah is a sought after keynote speaker and media contributor. He coaches athletes, celebrities, and high achievers in becoming emotionally fit, mentally tough, and socially responsible. He lives in Greenville, SC with his wife Renea, and has two kids- Jaheim & Maji.

You can follow him at:

www.Facebook.com/JemiahBattle

www.Twitter.com/MrEQfitness

Instagram @MrEQfitness

 To learn more about him and his initiatives visit WWW.JemiahBattle.com

# Introduction

I often get to talk to a lot of people whose lives are not working, relationships are failing or non-existent at all, and who have a deep inner turmoil & longing, a sense of unfulfillment. I can relate. I grew up like many boys in my generation, in a single-mother household of 6 without a positive male role model or any strong social structures. This environment made me an overachiever, and very determined to succeed to not become a neighborhood statistic. I believed that if better was possible, good wasn't good enough. I focused on learning every strategy in business & leadership, worked & grinded 24/7, and strived to never settle for mediocrity. This seemingly was a great mindset and strategy to have except for only 1 problem: I was starving myself emotionally and I was socially deprived. Both my Mom and Dad suffered from Mental Illness & Manic Depression, so it was natural for me to follow. Not being taught how to be resilient, or build healthy relationships, left me socially and emotionally unfit as a grown man. I was seemingly successful on the outside, but emotionally unfit & obese on the inside.

Then in 2010, my world, as I knew it, crashed. I lost both of my salaried jobs, had a couple of investment properties in foreclosure, and had just broke up with my then girlfriend. My bank accounts was soon depleted and I lost everything I had worked so hard for. I fell into a deep depression and mental stupor. Then something happened. On the brink of almost losing my sanity, God spoke to me clearly. He explained to me that I never took the "inner journey." I never developed my character. My values were based on street values, a street mindset...and that's it. I never developed a global perspective. I never developed my inner man, my inner story. So, through daily emotional fitness tools, inner soul workouts, and deep Identity-development I developed and redefined my state, my story, and my strategy. I became a student of the capacity of the human soul-my mind, my will, and my emotions. I developed healthy relationships and accountability. I became Socially & Emotionally Fit$^{TM}$. I became SELF Fit$^{TM}$. I spent so much of my life being emotionally obese, mishandling relationships, and "reacting" wrongly vs. "responding" correctly to life's situations, that I'm able to automatically connect with others in those areas. Now as a National Speaker and Certified Life & EQ Coach, I have made it my mission to teach and train others to do the same. To take the wheel of their life back from "emotional-hijackers" and truly become Emotionally Fit and Socially Responsible for the Game of Life, and shape their life around their Identity!

Everyone wants their lives to work again, or for some, even begin to work, but they don't see the problem. When I ask them to describe what they think is wrong, all I hear about is other people. Other people disappoint them. Or scare them. Then I hear about circumstance. The competition. The economy. The game. Their location. You get my drift. I know right away why their lives aren't working because I was once just like them. "A life of expectation of others is a life of disappointment." I would apologize for my seeming direct language, but I love you too much to sugar-coat anything in this book. So, please, stay with me. A life of trying to win the approval of others is a life of fear. My job as a coach is to restore the creative life. A creative life is a life of action and huge energy for achieving large and small goals, getting mass results; a life of systematic flow. It's never your life that's not working. It's always you. But that's the best news there could ever be. When God commanded us to take dominion, it wasn't over each other, but over ourselves. And that my friend is a Process! Say this with me, "I am a Process, not a Project!" This saying will make sense as you continue to read this book. Since God cannot tempt us, He put inside each and every one of us the ability to go through the process and become the person of greatness that we were created to be from the inside out! Everything, all true sustainable change comes from being clear. One of the goals of this book is to empower you to be clear. There are forms of coaching everywhere. Why not make it conscious and deliberate? For example, in Alcohol Anonymous classes, at the beginning of the 12 step meetings, they have a mantra that I want you to adapt while reading this book. Read aloud with me:

"If we are painstaking, about this phase of our development, we will be amazed before we are halfway through. We are going to know a new freedom and a new happiness. We will not regret the past nor wish to shut the door on it. We will comprehend the word serenity and we will know peace. No matter how far known the scale we have gone, we will see how our experience can benefit others. That feeling of uselessness and self-pity will disappear. We will lose interest in selfish things and gain interest in our fellows. Self-seeking will slip away. Our whole attitude and outlook upon life will change. Fear of people and of economic insecurity will leave us. We will intuitively know how to handle situations that use to baffle us. We will suddenly realize that God is doing for us what we could not do for ourselves. Are these extravagant promises? We think not. They are being fulfilled among us-sometimes quickly, sometimes slowly. They will always materialize if we work for them.

# PROCESS YOU to SUCCESS

One of the major reasons why we fail to find happiness or to create unique lifestyles is because we have not yet mastered the art of being.

While we are home, our thoughts are still absorbed with solving the challenges we face at school or the office. And when we are at school or the office, we find ourselves worrying about problems at home. We go through the day without really listening to what others are saying to us. We might be hearing the words, but we aren't absorbing the message.

As we go through the day, we find ourselves focusing on past experiences or future possibilities. We are so involved in yesterday and tomorrow that we never even notice that today is slipping by. We go through the day rather than getting something from the day. We are everywhere at any given moment in time—except living in that moment.

Lifestyle is learning to be wherever you are. It is developing a unique focus on the current moment, drawing from it all of the substance and wealth of experience and emotions that it has to offer. Lifestyle is taking time to watch a sunset. It is listening to silence. It is capturing each moment so that it becomes a new part of what we are now and what we are in the process of becoming. Lifestyle is not something we do—it is something we experience. And until we learn to be there, we will never master the art of living well.

I don't believe in sugarcoating the issues or dancing around the solutions, nor was I taught to do so, so, I will always attempt to give you answers up front and plainly. Success is the ability, 1$^{st}$, to recognize opportunity; 2$^{nd}$ to form plans and strategies that leverage opportunity; and 3$^{rd}$ to develop the necessary skills needed to execute those strategies. This book is just a brief insight into the process and journey I've took and continue to take myself through, as well as a few of the exercises that  I coach my clients into executing.  The information contained in this book is not new information. I just care about you enough to give it to you clearly. These are exercises that I have used and continue to practice faithfully. They are gathered from some of the most incredible, impactful people and ideas in the world. Let's go in….

# What exactly is Social & Emotional Living + Fitness ?

Research has proven that disciplined, focused practice can literally change our brains and our ability to create and sustain effective relationships. Simple, disciplined practice can be transformational! Emotional Fitness is rooted in Emotional Intelligence, or EQ. Emotional Intelligence is the capacity to create positive outcomes in relationship with others and with ourselves. It is the practice of being aware, understanding, and appropriately expressing and handling emotional states. Skills in Emotional Fitness can be acquired, practiced, and developed at any point in our lives.

Emotional Intelligence is a set of emotional and social skills that influence the way we perceive and express ourselves, develop and maintain social relationships, cope with challenges, and use emotional information in an effective and meaningful way.

While emotional intelligence isn't the sole predictor of human performance and development potential, it is proven to be a key indicator in those areas. Emotional intelligence is not a static factor— to the contrary, one's emotional intelligence changes over time and can be developed in targeted areas.

Emotional Intelligence can be applied to every situation, conversation, and setting. It will even help with those conversations you have with yourself. The beauty of EQ is that it can constantly be made stronger, unlike cognitive intelligence (IQ), which remains static over time. This is where Emotional Fitness comes into play.

People who are emotionally fit and healthy are in control of their emotions and their behavior. They are able to handle life's challenges, build strong relationships, and recover from setbacks. But just as it requires effort to build or maintain physical health, so it is with mental and emotional health. Improving your emotional health can be a rewarding experience, benefiting all aspects of your life, including boosting your mood, building resilience, and adding to your overall enjoyment of life. The sections in the book that are highlighted, please pay close attention to.

Emotional Fitness is the bridge between our dreams and our realities. There are three elements that affect the long-term success or failure of a person and whether they break through or not. For example, there are hundreds or even thousands of strategies out there for losing weight, and frankly most of them are proven to work—if you work them! We're not hurting for strategies. There are fitness clubs on every street, dieticians, health coaches, training videos, audios, books, etc. Yet 65% of the United States is overweight and 33% is obese, and those numbers are only growing geometrically. I would suggest to you that the problem for most people is not that they don't have a strategy—it's that they're not using a strategy that works for them or acting upon it. Why? Because they have a disempowering STORY., then once they create a better story, they still get caught and trapped in negative states of mind. So, let's work through these exercises together to truly shed the weight of

Emotional Obesity.-Know Yourself (Your State), CHOOSE Yourself (Your Story), and GIVE Yourself (Your Strategy). **Awareness**: Tuning into emotional data. **Management**: Responding intentionally. **Direction**: Leading purposefully. This my friends is a "Process," not a "Project." We treat our lives like a project most of the time because we hate the pain of taking ourselves through processes. The process is where we are refined and molded. Our lives are a result of the choices we have made based on the habits that we have. Our habits are part of a system that we each operate in. We often make the mistake of trying to treat our systems like a "project" and change from the outside. You change a system from the inside out. You can't by the "Process." Our lives are the result of a flow of a system that was probably forced on us at an early age. The beauty is that we can create a new system by creating new habits, and not only understanding the process, but actually having the tools to take ourselves through it! Emotional Fitness is needed to go through the processes of life. How many times have we gotten in our own way? Emotional Obesity is real! Most people are more concern with their physical weight and appearance, but still are suffering from emotional baggage and weight. Emotional weight causes stress, depression, anxiety, fear, failed relationships, poor judgement, poor decision making, and so many more ailments. Make sure that you grab a journal & notebook as you read this book. Let's start your journey & Process to being emotionally fit and socially responsible! Are you ready?

# Getting Rid of The Victim Mentality

"Victim" is learned helplessness and it can be unlearned. I think it's important to realize that many of those who have a victim mentality got there because of a traumatic experience, so they may have fear around personal interactions and feel powerless to know how to avoid future trauma. They need skills which will give them confidence they can create a life that doesn't have the kind of situations that created the feeling of being a victim. I teach my clients how to have and enforce personal boundaries and how to ask for what they want and say no to what they don't want. I also address beliefs that have been generated by what we tell ourselves what certain life experiences mean. The first aspect of emotional fitness is self-awareness about one's own feelings. Many victims are experts at how they think others are feeling (because studying, say an abuser, for clues something bad was getting ready to go down was one way they created personal safety). At the same time, many victims are completely out of touch with how THEY are feeling. Numbing is part of being a "victim". Knowing and taking responsibility for your own emotions and having the skills to create a life that generates healthy emotions is the key to moving past feeling like a victim.

I have found the ladder of accountability and power of a positive "no" to be two very helpful tools to move into choice and empowerment over thoughts and actions. Reinforcement of positive experiences and feelings is critical to overcoming past trauma and the feelings and perpetual thoughts associated with that trauma.

I have found that when coaching people with a victim mentality that accentuating the positive things that they have done, and explaining to them the strength that it takes to accomplish those things while carrying such a heavy burden upon their shoulders, proves that in many ways they are stronger than those who have not felt the sting of victimization. Victim mentality is an intellectual handicap, and often just getting out of bed is a victory. Focusing on the accumulation of "small wins" and seeing how that those small wins are relatively large wins compared to those without the victim mindset. Once you see that, start counting the small wins, and seeing how quickly they accumulate, then they will become big wins (in an avalanche) style. The victim will gain "victory momentum" and defeat their perceived villain (in the victim, victor, villain) triangle. Thus you will get stronger…"Grittier"…

# The Power of G.R.I.T. and Mental Toughness

*"I CAN'T MAKE YOU A CHAMPION, BUT I CAN TEACH YOU HOW TO THINK LIKE ONE!*

*-JIM FANNIN*

Life, relationships, our careers, sports, or any endeavor that we are trying to be great in should be an adventure; to be savored from beginning to end. They both are a game of constantly changing odds, constantly developing challenges, constantly opening opportunities.

To win either, you have to play. Sitting on the sidelines won't do. Even after you've achieved all you ever hoped to achieve, it's no time to stop living. This requires "mental toughness."

Mental Toughness is having the ability to be able to make the right personal, social, and professional decisions. Say for instance in the game of sports, most athletes are controlled by their urges, instincts and unrealistic desires. Having the ability to be mentally tough enough to take control of their urges, instincts and unrealistic desires is learned over time. Like attending class but not mentally prepared, making the decision not to attend the frat party the night before a game, studying for a test days before not the night before, keeping your cool when having a disagreement with your girlfriend,

18

having the ability to leave your entitlement ego in your dorm room while on campus are just a few of the areas of mental toughness in action.

At some point in this country we had G.R.I.T.-Guts, Resilience, Initiative, and Tenacity. We can google countless stories of men and women who dropped out of high school, people with "c" averages, and so on, who still achieved extraordinary levels of success. How did they do it? They possessed GRIT!

Grit is the tendency to sustain interest in an effort toward very long-term goals (Duckworth et al., 2007). Self-control is the voluntary regulation of behavioral, emotional, and intentional impulses in the presence of momentarily gratifying temptations or diversions (Duckworth & Seligman, 2005; Duckworth & Steinburg). On average, individuals who are gritty are more self-controlled.

Anybody can possess GRIT (I provide a GRIT assessment in my workbook "The Blueprint for Mental Toughness™ available on Amazon.com or at TheSELFinitiative.com). Dyson vacuum cleaners had 3,126 prototypes that fail before they found the right model. Nothing propels success better than failures! Why are we scared to fail? Why are we scared to let our kids fail?

*"Do it Scared!"*

-*Pastor Wendell Jones*


People don't see that dealing with "problems" and "challenges" is going to make them healthier and stronger and better as a human being. It's like lifting a weight. The arms strengthen and the weight feels progressively lighter. Dance with challenges until the challenges are too tired to stay any longer. Challenging yourself gives you a relationship that's beneficial. You begin to see it as something that serves you and feeds you and gives you energy and strengths. The more I challenge myself, the less the outside world throws things at me that "look" like obstacles and huge problems that are hard to overcome. The challenges then look easy. You've got to maintain focus under all circumstances. Whether it's the competition trying to break your composure, or you're hurting from fatigue or the conditions are unfavorable, you must stay focused. A winning mindset is teachable.

I coach and train athletes, so let's use them as an example. Similar to the physical part of the game, it'll be easier for some athletes and take more effort from others. But it's not a birthright. A winning mindset is something you practice and train for. With a winning mindset you possess the capability of willing yourself to win. Instead of caving into the pressure, you'll rise up to the challenge because you trained for those high pressure moments. Focus your attention on solutions, know your strengths, and use your winning mindset to bring out the fearless competitor within. Be in the present. Get your success. Don't spend one minute dreaming about it! When you do wake up, get to work! I think that's one reason I prefer to live on the east coast vs. the west coast. By the time someone wakes up in sunny California, they're already three hours behind the person grinding in New York. If you want your dreams to become reality, wake up!

*"I never spent one minute dreaming about success, but instead, I worked for it!"*

*-Estee Lauder*

Being emotionally fit is so important to your success. It allows you to be like Bamboo-flexible, adaptable, agile-ready for any storm or obstacle. Grit and mental toughness have no expiration date. GRIT is humanities grand equalizer.

This book is broke into 3 sections, with individual chapters and topics to help you become "emotionally fit and mentally tough for the game of life™." After each section I want you to journal what you plan to do with the information (You can purchase Process YOU™ Journals on Amazon.com or at www.TheSELFinitiative.com). Success is not what you hear, but what you do. Set time aside to study and meditate over what you read. With each new revelation and every piece of clarity that you receive ask yourself how am I going to A.C.T- what am I going to Apply, what am I going to Change, and what am I going to Teach. I will have reminders at the end of every section. There will also be a scannable QR code at the end of each major section that will send you to a motivational video that will engage you. If you don't have a QR scanner on your smart phone or tablet here are some links to download them: (www.qrstuff.com), (https://scan.me/download), or you can visit your App Store on ITunes, Google Play, or The Microsoft Store. Your first video is below. Ask yourself what are you going to do, what are you going to dump, and what are you going to delegate. Seek clarity. Prioritize! What is the most important thing that you need to do NOW? Not tomorrow, for tomorrow will have its own anxieties, but what are you going to do NOW!

The secret to winning and healing is taking action. Bold, no matter the size, ACTION! Let's get to work!

# PHASE I

# KNOW YOURSELF

# Recognizing emotions and dealing with Emotional Triggers

"How are you feeling?" We usually ask that question about a person's physical health, yet it's an equally valid question to ask about a person's emotional state of being. Each of us has an emotional state of well-being that is just as vital to our overall wholeness as our physical or spiritual well-being. You cannot be a whole person if you are in bondage to your emotions or in denial of them.

I meet many people, famous and not, who try to deny that they have an emotional response to the situations that they encounter. They seem to believe that it is weak for a person to cry, a flaw for a person to feel anger or to express disappointment, a lack of self-control for a person to laugh aloud. Such people are missing out on the fullness of what it means to be alive.

An expression of emotion is part of what makes us human. Emotions are a gift of God, who created each of us with a capacity to feel and express emotions. Even God has emotions! Whether you believe in God or not, we all have heard "Jesus wept." Furthermore, emotions are vital to our ability to communicate to others the uniqueness of our personalities. They are means of responding to others and well, life in general.

Many people don't know how to express their emotions in healthful ways that promote good relationships with friends and family members. Learning how to deal with one's emotions is a vital skill, knowing how to direct them toward good outcomes, express them without missing the mark or goal, and give voice to emotions in order to improve communication.

Still other people allow themselves to have a free-flowing emotional response to life, and they have learned to control their emotions, but they are uncomfortable talking about the way they feel. Learning how to tell others what you are feeling is a part of becoming a mature person. It is a skill that is critical to the development of adult-to-adult relationships. Emotional Fitness is our social responsibility to this world. It is our responsibility and our privilege to express love through our emotions, not hide them. Take note MEN: It is a **Privilege** to **Express** love. It is exercising Divine authority at it's finest!

Wherever you are on the spectrum of emotional growth-from denial to full expression- I want you to have optimum emotional health and be emotionally fit for the game of life. I want you to express emotions in the way that you were created to express them. I want you to freely admit to emotions, to know how to control them and use them in right ways, and to discuss your emotional responses with others, especially those you say you love.

Are there good and bad emotions? Yes and no. Emotions in themselves are neutral. Their expression takes on a nature of good and bad. All emotions are valid. Each has a place in God's design of your human psyche and spirit. Your emotions were created that you might enjoy them and communicate them.

Each person is going to have a unique response to life's

situations, problems, and challenges. One person may weep at the beauty of a moving piece of music (Stevie Wonder does it to me every time!), another person may sit in silent awe, and still another person may stand to give thunderous applause. We must allow others the privilege of their expression.

We also must give one another the privilege of expressing emotions privately. I advocate the healthful and free expression of emotions, yet I do not advocate that a person be required to express emotions in the presence of others.

Conversely, we must be careful not to assume that we have the right to express our emotions freely and fully in the presence of others. Every public expression of emotion should take into consideration the people witnessing the emotional display. This is where social awareness and social responsibility can come into play.

Sometimes we are overcome with emotion. We may lose control in a particular situation. At those times, we may feel that we should apologize for our lack of restraint, but we should never apologize for having feelings. When we apologize for having emotions, we are in danger of stuffing them, with a possible eruption later. This is what we see play out in professional sports, domestic violence cases, and unhealthy relationships. It's not that the person is crazy or even violent. It's that we never know the depth of how long or how deep someone has been stuffing and compartmentalizing their emotions. This is extremely true for men. We are taught at an early age to "show no emotion," "crying is for sissies," "stop being a wimp…" etc, etc. When in reality, the young male is becoming more and more emotionally obese and socially unhealthy. I've seen that most men who commit physical acts of domestic violence, have themselves been victims of verbal, social and emotional abuse in some form or fashion for years. This doesn't excuse their violent behavior, but it should give us another baseline for dealing with batterers and offenders. They don't have a violence problem, they have an emotional fitness problem! Point blank: Stuffed emotions can be damaging and will explode, often always erupting in the wrong circumstance.

Sadly, lots of achievers who know how to accomplish most of what they want to get out of life, but they don't know how to take care of themselves emotionally. They end up burning up most of their emotional resources and losing momentum.

We see others who really care about making progress in some areas of their lives but instead of moving forward, they see themselves moving sideways. Some emotional reaction is pulling them off track. Something is distracting them taking them further away from the results that they are seeking. If this is you, just say "ouch," take heed, and keep moving forward. Forward is the only direction. Taking action is the only way to get fit in any area of life, especially as it pertains to emotional fitness. And here's the kicker- the distraction is internal. Here's what I've learned. When things are going crazy in our external world, we go crazy trying to change things in our external world. In Steven Covey's book "The 7 Habits of Highly Effective People," he points out that this is actually down the line in our actions. One of the first action steps is to put first things first and reflect. When things are going crazy in our outside world, it is then that we need to take the "inner" journey. When things are going crazy in the inside of us (anxiety, fear, worry, etc.) we need to take action. Healing comes as we walk. If we don't take the inner journey, it affects our confidence and joy and makes us unable to enjoy emotional peaks. Remember what's important in low times, regardless of external circumstances. So how do you manage your internal state so that you have the external results you want- and so you can enjoy the results? Most "successful" people aren't happy. Most aren't experiencing true joy and peace. True joy and peace comes from knowing and you are and authentically being that person. Not that you won't have emotional highs and lows, but that you become emotionally fit enough to be aware of your emotional triggers; those things that causes you to act and behave outside of your values and character that YOU stated and that YOU committed to being.

- What do you want more of in your life?
- What emotions do you want to experience?

-If you express more joy, you attract more joy.

-If you express more peace, you'll attract more peace.

-If you exude more trust, confidence, and security in YOU, then you will attract more of the same.

In ignoring our emotional triggers, we set ourselves up for emotional obesity. We go to several extremes when we are emotionally obese. Let's talk about a few of them. One, for example, is that we mask it by appearing to be extra determined, having a false sense of humility, or trying to show everyone around us how serious we are. Doing this we will and often do burn ourselves out emotionally and totally ignore and neglect our internal outcomes. Or, we go the other extreme and starve ourselves emotionally. A lot of men do this one. This gives loss of enthusiasm, motivation, and inspiration. You start to forget your "why" (which we will discuss later in the book). You start to run out of energy and new ideas. This is not healthy. This is what I call "emotional starvation." This is where you start to eat "fear" for food, versus making "fear" and/or pain work for your good. A third extreme that many live in while emotionally obese is the "Self-Rescue" mode. They say things like, "This is so hard. I need a break. I need some kindness. Let me_____, just once." One word: Compromise. We compromise our values, our vision, our identities, our morals, our souls. We try to "self-rescue" ourselves from our decisions. Your body has a safety mechanism that will try to bail you out. In this mode you are so burnt out that you are operating off pure emotions. The comfort and soothing you crave vs. what's emotionally healthy for your soul. Backsliding; probably in the same area that you're trying so hard to be disciplined in.

Don't hold yourself hostage emotionally…

Emotionally when you say, "I'll feel happier later when____," you are telling yourself that it is impossible to be happy today. Your psychology system is being starved for rewards, and you're psychology system have to fed daily! As with the physical body, so is the same with the inner body, "You are what you eat!" This not only emotionally unhealthy, it is mentally dangerous on so many levels. Top achievers know that they have to put themselves into a pleasurable mode of winning first so that they can hopefully achieve results later. The trick is that you have to feel like a winner from the beginning to actually win later. This can be done by being emotionally fit.

- Are you aware of your emotional triggers?
- Are you aware of your emotional reactions?

Becoming emotionally fit will give you the energy, focus, stamina, and healthy rewards to enable you to achieve more and enjoy the journey. You just have to "Say Yes to the Process!" It all begins with self- awareness…

PROCESS YOU to SUCCESS

# Self-Awareness

*"To be Aware is to be Alive"*

"It is in quiet that our best ideas occur to us. Don't make the mistake of believing that by a frantic kind of dashing around you are being your most effective and efficient self. Don't assume that you are wasting time when you take time out for thought." – Napoleon Hill and W. Clement Stone

Everyone, especially the older one gets, wants a peace of mind. Whether you are an athlete, celebrity, business man (woman), or just an individual facing the pressures of everyday life…you want a peace of mind. But most of us, if we are really being honest to ourselves, experience more stress and frustration than peace.

Question: Are you investing in yourself? If you don't grow, how do you expect the people around you to grow? How familiar are you with stress? How familiar are you with frustration? Let's start off with a quick quiz. Complete the following sentences with a true word of where you are currently or where you have been recently, and say it aloud:

I am ready to throw in the_____.

I am at the end of my_____.

I am just a hand full of_____.

I'm at my wit's_____.

# PROCESS YOU to SUCCESS

I feel like resigning from_____.

I can't win for_____.

That's just my_____.

I go two steps forward, just to get knocked two
steps_____

How did you feel saying these things? How did you fare out? If
you answered towel, rope, nerves, apart, or race, you made an A+.
Congratulations, you have a Ph. D in stress! Most of us have
mumbled these sayings sub-consciously, almost by second nature.

Stress and frustration are, sadly, part of our modern culture.
Everybody is tense, on edge, in a rush....unaware. Sales of
tranquilizers, anti-depressants, aspirins, and alcoholic beverages are at
an all time high. People just want to disconnect from their world,
when in reality, we only just want a peace of mind. We want
emotional peace with ourselves, and relational peace with every in
our lives-especially loved ones. Yep, relational peace is included. For
a lot of us, we would say that most of our problems are people
problems: An aggravating boss, lazy or complaining teammates,
annoying co-worker, nagging significant others, relatives, and the list
could go on and on. We have to deal with conflict, competition,
pettiness, and criticism on a pretty regular basis-especially if you are
in a leadership position! These things can rob us of our peace. But
can I let you in on a little secret (there will be several in this book):
Nobody can "rob" us of peace, we choose to give it to them. The
reason for this is true peace comes from within. True peace comes
from the quiet confidence and personal power of KNOWing
yourself, knowing your value, and knowing who you are. When you
truly know your intrinsic value, which is immeasurable by the way, it
becomes harder to let others put a price on your peace. If you own a

million dollar mansion with priceless items in the inside of it, buried treasure underneath it, would you allow anyone to come and tell you what "they feel" the house is worth? Absolutely not! So why do we allow people, relationships, the media, society tell us who we are?

The first step to knowing yourself, and really being the driver of this journey called life, you must take the inner journey. Truly knowing yourself and becoming emotionally fit starts with self-awareness.

Self-Awareness is defined as noticing and being able to label your feelings, emotions, —gut-levell instincts or reactions; being able to connect these to their source; recognizing their effects on your mind and your body; using your feelings as a valuable source of insight and information about yourself, others and the situations around you.

People with this skill

- Know which emotions they are feeling and why

- Realize, in the moment, the links between their feelings and what they think, do and say

- Recognize how their feelings affect their performance

- Are able to articulate their feelings and appropriately express them

- Can tell – in the moment – when they are getting upset

People lacking this skill

- May receive messages from their bodies such as chronic headaches, lower back pain, neck or shoulder pain, heart racing, sweaty palms, anxiety attacks or other signals, but generally don't pay attention to these signals or connect them to their source, to what's causing these physical symptoms

- Fail to gain insight and information from what their bodies might be trying to tell them

- Get irritated, frustrated or angry easily, causing them to treat people in an abrasive way

- Fail to see that what they are doing or being asked to do might not be aligned with their personal goals and values

- Often feel stressed and out of balance in terms of their work life, health and family

# Understanding the 6 Human needs

One of my mentors from afar, the great Tony Robbins, helped me to truly understand how a lot of our foundation for our actions are based in our basic 6 human needs, and our awareness and self-actualization of them.

I see it all the time, in the sports world and out-people can equate their net worth with their self worth. Their identity is married so deeply to their bank statements and game stats that they've forgotten that money is simply a vehicle for trying to meet our needs, almost all of which are not financial. We're all familiar with the saying that money cannot buy happiness, but I'm convinced that almost everybody has to learn that lesson the hard way because let's face it; the idea of having enough money to throw at your problems until they're solved is a seductive impulse.

It certainly was something I constantly thought about as a kid. Growing up, money was always out of reach. It was always a source of stress because there was never enough of it. Then, when I changed my perspective, I found joy in serving and giving. Once I start serving and being committed to something bigger than myself and my immediate needs, my value raised, and money along with the strategy to make it, came! . I'd learned the joy of giving and to this day I consider contribution to be one of the six most important things every person needs.

Whatever emotion you're after, whatever vehicle you pursue—being the greatest athlete, building a business, getting married, raising a family, traveling the world—whatever you think your life's mission is, there are six basic, universal needs that make us tick and drive all human behavior. Combined, they are the force behind the crazy things (other) people do and the great things we do. ;) We all have the same six needs, but how we value those needs and in what order, determines the direction of our life.

## Need 1: Certainty/Comfort

The first human need is the need for Certainty. It's our need to feel in control and to know what's coming next so we can feel secure. It's the need for basic comfort, the need to avoid pain and stress, and also to create pleasure. Our need for certainty is a survival mechanism. It affects how much risk we're willing to take in life—in our jobs, in our investments, and in our relationships. The higher the need for certainty, the less risk you'll be willing to take or emotionally bear. By the way, this is where your real "risk tolerance" comes from.

## Need 2: Uncertainty/Variety

Let me ask you a question: Do you like surprises? If you answered "yes," you're kidding yourself! You like the surprises you want. The ones you don't want, you call problems! But you still need them to put some muscle in your life. You can't grow muscle—or character—unless you have something to push back against.

## Need 3: Significance

We all need to feel important, special, unique, or needed. So how do some of us get significance? You can get it by earning billions of dollars, or collecting academic degrees—distinguishing yourself with a master's or a PhD. You can build a giant Twitter following. Or you can go on The Bachelor or become the next Real Housewife of Orange County. Some do it by putting tattoos and piercings all over themselves and in places we don't want to know about. You can get significance by having more or bigger problems than anybody else. "You think your husband's a dirt bag, take mine for a day!" Of course, you can also get it by being more spiritual (or pretending to be).

Spending a lot of money can make you feel significant, and so can spending very little. We all know people who constantly brag about their bargains, or who feel special because they heat their homes with cow manure and sunlight. Some very wealthy people gain significance by hiding their wealth. Like the late Sam Walton, the founder of Wal-Mart and for a time the richest man in America, who drove around Bentonville, Arkansas, in his old pickup, demonstrating he didn't need a Bentley—but of course, he did have his own private fleet of jets standing by.

Significance is also a money maker—that's where my dear friend Steve Wynn has made his fortune. The man who made Las Vegas what it is today knows people will pay for anything they believe is "the best," anything that makes them feel special, unique or important, anything that makes them stand out from the crowd. He provides the most exclusive, luxurious experiences imaginable in his casinos and hotels—they are truly magnificent and unmatched in the world.

**Need 4: Love & Connection**

The fourth basic need is Love and Connection. Love is the oxygen of life; it's what we all want and need most. When we love completely we feel alive, but when we lose love, the pain is so great that most people settle on connection, the crumbs of love. You can get that sense of connection or love through intimacy, or friendship, or prayer, or walking in nature. If nothing else works, you can get a dog.

These first four needs are what I call the needs of the personality. We all find ways to meet these—whether by working harder, coming up with a big problem, or creating stories to rationalize them. The last two are the needs of the spirit. These are even more rare and not everyone meets these. When these needs are met, we truly feel fulfilled.

**Need 5: Growth**

If you're not growing, you're dying. If a relationship is not growing, if a business is not growing, if you're not growing, it doesn't matter how much money you have in the bank, how many friends you have, how many people love you—you're not going to experience real fulfillment. And the reason we grow, I believe, is so we have something of value to give.

**Need 6: Contribution**

Corny as it may sound, the secret to living is giving. Life's not about me; it's about we. Think about it, what's the first thing you do when you get good or exciting news? You call somebody you love and share it. Sharing enhances everything you experience.

Life is really about creating meaning. And meaning does not come from what you get, it comes from what you give. Ultimately it's not what you get that will make you happy long term, but rather who you become and what you contribute will.

Now think about how money can fulfill the six human needs. Can money give us certainty? You bet. Variety? Check. Obviously it can make us feel important or significant. But what about connection and love? In the immortal words of the Beatles, money can't buy you love. But it can buy you that dog! And it can, unfortunately, give you a false sense of connection because it attracts relationships, although not always the most fulfilling kind. How about growth? Money can fuel growth in business and in learning. And the more money you have, the more you can contribute financially.

But here's what I truly believe: if you value Significance above all else, money will always leave you empty unless it comes from a contribution you've made. And if you're looking for significance from money, it's a high price to pay. You're looking for big numbers but it's unlikely you'll find big fulfillment.

The ultimate significance in life comes not from something external, but from something internal. It comes from a sense of esteem for ourselves, which is not something we can ever get from someone else. People can tell you you're beautiful, smart, intelligent, the best, or they can tell you that you are the most horrible human being on earth—but what matters is what you think about yourself. Whether or not you believe that deep inside you are continuing to grow and push yourself, to do and give more than was comfortable or you even thought possible. The wealthiest person on earth is one who appreciates.

1. *Which of these six needs do you tend to focus on or value the most?*

2. *What are the ways (good and bad) you meet these needs? For example, in your relationships, work, eating, exercise, etc.?*

3. *How can you increase your focus on growth and contribution? What are some things you can do, or new experiences you can participate in?*

# Your values

If you don't know who you are, then how can you decide what to do? How can you formulate values, adopt beliefs, or establish rules? How can you judge whether something is good, bad, or indifferent? The biggest challenge for someone who perceives his identity as a drug addict is: What does he change his identity to? To a "recovering drug addict?" This doesn't change his identity; it merely describes the state he's in currently. "Drug-free" doesn't do it either, because most see it as a temporary state—and it still focuses on drugs as one of the ways of defining oneself. When this person develops the conviction that he is absolutely clean, that he's now a "Christian," "Muslim," "Jew," or "Buddhist,""Celebrity" "Pro-Athlete" or now that he's a "leader"—or anything else other than a "drug addict"—that's when his behavior changes. As we develop new beliefs about who we are, our behavior will change to support the new identity.   People who act inconsistently with who they believe they are set the stage for the societal cliché of an "identity crisis." When the crisis hits, they are immediately disoriented, questioning their previous convictions. Their whole world is turned upside down, and they experience an intense fear of pain. This is what happens to so many people having a "midlife crisis." Often people identify themselves as being young, and that some environmental stimulant—turning a certain age, comments from friends, graying hair— causes them to dread their approaching years and the new, less desirable identity that they expect to experience with it. Thus, in a desperate effort to maintain their identity, they do things to prove they're still young: buy fast cars, change their hairstyles, divorce their spouses, change jobs. If those who had this issue had a solid grasp of their true identities, would they experience this crisis at all? I suspect not. Having an identity that is specifically linked to your age or how you look would definitely set you up for pain because these things will change. If we have a broader sense of "who" we are, our identity never becomes threatened.

Whether you have an empowering story or disempowering one is influenced most powerfully by the mental and emotional STATE you're in at this moment in time. As human beings we all develop emotional patterns—moods—that are mental or emotional states that tend to filter how we look at our lives. The states we go into most often then become the most powerful filter of all that will determine whether we find the strategies necessary to succeed and whether we come up with a story that will empower us. The big question then becomes, what is it that we can do to change our state of mind when we're not able to maximize our true potential? For people who are experiencing stress at any given moment, a form of relief can be to simply change your physiology— take a couple of deep breaths. Most people only use 20% of their lung capacity taking small short breaths, but 70% of the body's toxins can actually be released when taking a full breath! By taking the time to fill your lungs and release you can not only improve your health but also radically decrease the anxiety related to that moment. There are many ways to change your physiology and in our seminars we prove this time after time by taking people who feel depressed and having them make a radical shift. Intuitively we know this can be changed not only by the way we move, but our breath and body temperature as well.

The second thing that affects our state is what we focus on. For example, if you've been at a funeral honoring someone you cared about and everyone is in a sad state and afterwards someone shares a story or anecdote about something that person did that was extremely humorous, suddenly everyone goes from tears to laughter. In an instant our states can be changed by what we focus on. What's wrong is always available—but so is what's right. Whatever we focus on affects our state and our state then effects the story we have about who we are, what's life about, what's possible and what's not. From that story we will often determine whether or not we will maximize our capabilities and the strategies that will help us achieve what we're truly after in a sustainable way.

Learning to put yourself in a peak state consistently is one of the greatest gifts you can give yourself and your life. It can transform your stories and give you the strategies to breakthrough.

So take a moment to identify who you are. Who are you? There are so many ways in which we define ourselves. We may describe ourselves as our emotions (I'm a lover, I'm peaceful, I'm intense), our professions (I'm an attorney, I'm a doctor, I'm a priest), our titles (I'm Executive Vice-President), our incomes (I'm a millionaire), our roles (I'm a mother, I'm the eldest of five girls), our behaviors (I'm a gambler), our possessions (I'm a BMW owner), our metaphors (I'm king of the hill, I'm the low man on the totem pole), our feedback (I'm worthless, I'm special), our spiritual beliefs (I'm Jewish), our looks (I'm beautiful, I'm ugly, I'm old), our accomplishments (I'm the 1960 Spring Valley High Homecoming Queen), our past (I'm a failure), and even what we're not (I'm not a quitter).

The identity that our friends and peers have tends to affect us as well. Take a good look at your friends. Who you believe they are is often a reflection of who you believe you are. If your friends are very loving and sensitive, there's a great chance that you see yourself in a similar vein. The timeframe you use to define your identity is very powerful as well. Do you look to your past, your present, or the future to define who you truly are? Years ago my present and past weren't terribly exciting, so I consciously fused my identity with the vision I had of who I knew I would become. I didn't have to wait; I began to live as this man now.

Take a deep breath and release it. Ask, "Who am I?"

I AM…

_____

I Am…

_____

I Am….

_____

I Am…

_____

I AM….

_____

I AM...

_____

I Am…

_____

I Am….

_____

I Am…

_____

I AM….

I know that wasn't easy! How did it feel? Was it empowering? "I Am" are two of the most powerful words that you will ever say. You are God's masterpiece. There is only 1 you in the entire universe! That means that your value far super-cedes any dollar amount. We disconnect from our original savage grace and creativity in the name of being accepted and liked and not embarrassing ourselves with peers. We sell out for approval. We grow p and try to get jobs and families like everybody else. We disconnect from our courage and our power. To reconnect, we have to understand the process. My Pastor once told me that if you know it, you can think it; and if you can think it, you can do it. You can do it!

To assist you in defining yourself, remember that identity is simply what distinguishes you from everyone else.

1.  If you were to look in the dictionary under your name, what would it say? Would three words just about cover it, or would your epic narrative consume page after page, or demand a volume of its own? Right now, write down the definition you would find if you were to look up your name in a dictionary. Take a moment, and let your answers sink in. When you're ready, move to the next exercise.

2.  2) If you were to create an ID card that would represent who you truly are, what would be on it—and what would you leave off? Would it include a picture or not? Would you list your vital statistics? Your physical description? Your accomplishments? Your emotions? Your beliefs? Your affiliations? Your aspirations? Your motto? Your abilities?

Take a moment to describe what would be on this identity card and what would be left off in order to show someone who you really are.

Now, take a look at what you've written down, at the descriptions you have of your identity—in essence, the story of your life. How do you feel about it? I hope you're taking a moment right now to really appreciate who you are, to feel the deep emotion that comes with recognition. If you're noticing that your identity creates pain, know that whatever you call your identity is simply what you've decided to identify with, and that in a moment you could change it all. You have the power within you right now. In fact, after looking at how identities evolve, you'll have an opportunity to expand your identity, and therefore your entire life.)

You might ask, "Isn't my identity limited by my experience?" No, it's limited by your interpretation of your experience. Your identity is nothing but the decisions you've made about who you are, what you've decided to fuse yourself with. You become the labels you've given yourself. The way you define your identity defines your life.

# 2 Subtle Problems that are Killing your dreams

The first one is doubt...

Doubt is a hidden insidious problem. When we were children we *responded and lived without doubt.*

But as we grew up we became educated about the *'likelihood' of something working out for us...* This knowledge today eats away at your dreams and desires...

It does it silently, hiding in the shadows and only occasionally showing itself to you so that you can see it... And when you see it *your ego wraps it up in the disguise of being a preventative benefit to you.*

So not only can you not see it, but you cannot see the harm it has done to you!

Now very quickly your ego will say to you, *"no, he's wrong... your doubt is helping you..."*

*"After all the 'likelihood' of it happening is so small that you do not want to get your hopes up and believe in something which will result in you feeling let down and not want to try again... do you?"*

Now within that there are a whole host of bugs which your ego can use to switch direction on you in a heartbeat...

This in turn, enables it to *prevent progress in the area of your life which you currently wish to get progress in.*

The problem is that these *'normal'* thoughts seem harmless and actually seem helpful!

They are hiding in plain sight and have in effect become invisible...

So you doubt something and you see this most of the time as a very good thing...

So how the heck are you ever going to be able to see a bug you see as good... in the reality of seeing it as bad?

*Simple answer is you can't...* Or it can take years to see this sort of thing happening and you overcoming invisible and *seemingly helpful doubt...*

Consider, *just what value do you feel it would be worth to your life to be able to see all doubt in all its guises as a bad thing?*

As always, if you can't see it then you can't fix it.

Now the problem is that until we become predominantly present and until we have trained our minds to seek out and dissolve any thoughts which take us against the direction we wish to go...

*...Then we will stand still in life, but have the illusion, thanks to our egos of making progress...*

So this subtle, invisible problem, which you *almost certainly see as a benefit is currently daily costing you progress, money, and life...*

But as you cannot see it and as you are currently misdirected by your ego to look elsewhere...

It means you definitely cannot fix it because you aren't looking, *or at the very best you are looking in the wrong place.*

Consider, *is it of benefit to me to spend time on discovering where I doubt things?* Avoid a yes or no answer, just consider this for a few moments...

Would you like to know the secret to invisibility & being victim to a subtle enemy?

Simple, it's misdirection, every magician/illusionist knows it as does every military tactician.

The purpose of military misdirection is to cause the opponent to stand still whilst gaining tactical strategic advantage...

And the best misdirection is when you have a spy in the camp convincing the opposing force that what they are doing is helping them.

*The secret to progress is truth and visibility,* <u>you have to know the truth and see what's really going on.</u>

So let's say you set up your desire, as an example for *'Financial Freedom.'*

*... You are saying you desire or want financial freedom, but at the same time you are doubting in some way that you'll achieve it...*

# PROCESS YOU to SUCCESS

*...And you have convinced yourself that you mustn't expect it to be easy, or expect to get too much money.*

So you are looking at being realistic as it's not likely you'll achieve it, so you're not wanting to get your hopes up too high... You are *managing* your expectations.

Or another example is, finding a person to be with, or to employ, or to go into business with... whatever... you name it!

If you doubt that you can find them and you tell yourself to be realistic because that's the logical thing to do otherwise you'll be let down and will look a fool in some way...

Then guess what you are creating in your mind...

You don't find the person, but your ego quickly tells you that you are not a fool and you were right to dare not to dream...

You don't get Financial Freedom, but now your ego quickly tells you that you are a fool and you knew you shouldn't get your hopes up... Now you should keep quiet otherwise other people will see you are fool.


*Do you see the insidious nature of your doubt?*

*Do you see how this invisible problem is killing your progress because you cannot see it's near continuous misdirection!*

As I said, it can take months or years of work to reveal to yourself your own self doubts...

It can take tens of thousands of words to reveal the invisible problems...

And now because *you 'know' that this invisible problem is this much of a problem…*

NOW your ego gets to use that too… As knowledge is not power, the correct application of knowledge is.

The nuances of this problem are quickly lost or overtaken by your life situation so you cannot fix them.

The secret is to learn exactly how to create the mind state around whatever you desire so that you can see it <u>has happened</u>. When you have seen that… Then you can see the invisible problem as it creeps up on you from any angle.

*Think about it…*

If you were able to cultivate your mind state to the point where it had happened for real in your mind (SO NO DOUBT AT ALL WAS PRESENT) and you were now just working diligently on bringing it into everyone else's reality…

*Then how would that feel…*

just consider how doubt is *probably killing your dreams and halting your progress*, by the way your ego tells you to be realistic, not get your hopes up…

Think about those two last statements a little: Be realistic – Don't get your hopes up

Do you know what those statements are?

They are what to think information that the *'what to think*
51

*world' has programmed into you...*

*How does that make you feel?*

The second invisible problem is self worth...

Self worth is a hidden insidious problem.

When we were children we responded and lived without any lack of self worth... *It simply did not exist.*

But as we grew up we became educated about *what another person thought we were doing wrong...* Then we began to allow this insidious invisible problem to eat away at our ability to create our dreams.

Because for some *hidden reason* we begin to think *we are not worthy of freedom, happiness, success, being a business owner, becoming rich...*

You name it, we end up considering *we are not worthy...*

A lack of self worth eats away at you silently...

It trains you to *keep quiet* otherwise those around you may find out that you *don't deserve to be there* and that you *are a fraud...*

Your ego doesn't want you to realize that you do deserve to be there! So it hides in the shadows and only occasionally shows itself to you...

When it does show it to you then it wraps up a lack of self worth in *the disguise of being a preventative benefit to you...* It's a right little b@st@rd!

So not only can you NOT see it, but you cannot see the harm it has and is doing to you.

Now very quickly your ego will say to you, *"No, he's wrong... he doesn't know that you don't really deserve to be there/here..."*

*"After all you have to keep this secret otherwise you will never have any chance of getting there... You mustn't let your guard down otherwise all you have done will be wasted!"*

Now again within that there are a whole host of bugs which your ego can use to switch direction on you in a heartbeat enabling it to prevent progress in the area of your life which you currently wish to get progress in.

The problem is that these *'normal'* thoughts which you are trained (programmed) to think are *dragging you down.*

You are programmed to think they *have to be there* and so allow them 'airtime' in your mind.

But *no thought stands still,* every thought is either helping you get where you desire to go or is hurting you.

Now if you are present then you can remember that... But if you are not then you will not and *you will allow yourself to continue to think destructive thoughts and sabotage your dreams.*

Now your ego uses this lack of self worth to sell you on the fact that this negative mindset is actually helpful to you!

…And in doing so converts this *visible problem* into an *invisible one!*

So you thinking you are not worthy of something actually has transmuted in a very mutated way into you seeing it as a good thing!

*So how the heck are you ever going to be able to see a bug which you see as good, which in reality is bad?*

Simple you can't…

Or it can take years to see this sort of thing happening and you overcoming invisible and seemingly helpful low self worth…

Consider, *what value do you feel it would be worth to your life to be able to let go of all current and future low self worth?*

Now the problem is that until we become predominantly present, and until we have trained our minds to seek out and dissolve any thoughts which take us against the direction we wish to go, *then we will stand still in life!*

But we have been sold the illusion, (thanks to our egos) of making progress…

So this invisible problem, which you almost certainly see as a benefit *is currently costing you progress, money, and life…*

But as *you cannot see it*, and as you are currently misdirected by your ego to *look elsewhere…* Meaning you cannot fix it as you aren't even looking, or at best *you are looking in the wrong place.*

## PROCESS YOU to SUCCESS

Remember what we said about invisibility? Which was *misdirection, (every magician/illusionist knows it as does every military tactician.)*

*The purpose of military misdirection is to cause the opponent to stand still whilst gaining tactical strategic advantage…*

*And the best misdirection is when you have a spy in the camp convincing the opposing force that what they are doing is helping them.*

*The secret to progress is truth and visibility, you have to know the truth and see what's really going on.'*

So let's say for example you set up your desire for *'Financial Freedom'.*

…But you are thinking *in any way,* that *you are not worthy of achieving it* and you have convinced yourself that *you mustn't expect it to happen,* or *expect to get too much money…*

So you are looking at being realistic as it's not likely you'll achieve it, so you're not wanting to get your hopes up too high… You are managing your expectations.

Or again for another example, finding a person to be with, or to employ, or to go into business with… whatever… you name it!

If you do not feel worthy of having any of these things happen and you tell yourself to *be realistic because that's the logical thing to do, otherwise you'll be let down and will look a fool in some way…*

Then guess what you are creating in your mind…

You don't find the person, but your ego quickly tells you that you are not a fool and you were right to dare not to dream... *As you were not worthy...* Therefore reinforcing *its correctness* and *your wrongness*

You don't get Financial Freedom, but now your ego quickly tells you that you are a fool and you knew you shouldn't get your hopes up... Now you should keep quiet otherwise other people will see you are fool...

Then it uses that next time to beat you up with some more...

*Do you see the insidious nature of any lack of self worth?*

*Do you see how this invisible problem is killing your progress because you cannot see it's near continuous misdirection?*

As I said, it can take months or years of work to reveal to yourself your own lack of self worth in a way which you will not continue to re-live it again and again.

It can take tens of thousands of words to reveal the invisible problem of low self worth, as anytime you do something new it will have another way of getting at you!

...And now because you *'know'* that this invisible problem is this much of a problem... NOW your ego gets to use that too...

Because knowledge is not power, the correct application of knowledge is.

The nuances of this problem are quickly lost or overtaken by your life situation *so you cannot fix them,* because your ego will currently be telling you that *"You know it now, and this is great!"*

*It's always there to keep you down with misdirection!*

## PROCESS YOU to SUCCESS

The secret is of course *to learn exactly how to create the mind state around whatever you desire so that you can see it has happened.* When you have seen that, *then you can see the invisible, subtle problem* as it creeps up on you from any angle.

How is your refusal in being honest with yourself giving you blind spots and allowing fear, doubt, and self-condemnation subtly, creep in your mind?

# Personal Power

Personal Power is defined as a sense of self-confidence and an inner knowing that you can meet life's challenges and live the life you choose; the ability to have the difficult conversations in life, and to speak your truth quietly, sincerely, assertively and appropriately

<u>People with this awareness</u>

- Have a calm inner conviction about who they are and their ability to get the things they want and need in life

- Believe they can set the direction of their lives, and do

- Are able to distinguish between the things they have control over in life and those they do not; and don't stress over the latter

- Define themselves from the inside out (—I'm capable,—I'm good at managing setbacks,—I'm pretty good at managing conflicts,—I'm creative) rather than from the outside in (—I'm a Vice President,—I'm a banker,—I'm a lawyer, or —I'm a doctor)

- Make things happen; don't believe in fate

- Feel in control of their lives

- Know what they want and go after it

- Are confident in their self

- Can speak their truth and give voice to their convictions

People who Lack this Awareness

- Avoid confrontations with people, even to get a problem resolved or when the confrontation might be best in the long run.

- Have difficulty speaking truth to power

- Lack confidence in their own judgment

- Avoid going to the heart of an issue

- Hesitate to try new things

- Have difficulty defending their ideas

- Avoid challenges, give in too readily

- Question their own ability; often feel powerless

- Don't take risks or chances, even moderate ones

- Are unable to set boundaries or demand respectful treatment from others

Take control of your consistent emotions and begin to consciously and deliberately reshape your daily experience of life. This gives you POWER. This puts you back in the driver seat and tells your emotions to get in the back and buckle up! Be without worry of things feeling right at first. Your emotions that you currently feel are based on situations and circumstances from your past. It may take a while for your emotions to catch up with your new perspective, so expect discomfort anytime you decide to make a change. Remember, you are in the driver's seat, not your emotion. You condition them to work for you! It is simply the beliefs that we use to define our own individuality, what makes us unique—good, bad, or indifferent—from other individuals. And our sense of certainty about who we are creates the boundaries and limits within which we live.

Development tips

- Make a list of the things you've accomplished in your life; make a sincere effort to recapture the feelings you experienced when you achieved your goals

- Identify the things you excel in, tap into the emotions associated with those strengths

- Examine the causes of your lack of confidence or lack of personal power, i.e., a lack of skill in a new position? If so, seek out formal or informal training to boost your confidence. Is it a lack of experience? Seek the help of a mentor who will provide you some guidance.

- Take an assertiveness course or read a book on assertiveness

- Become aware of communication circumstances when you put yourself down or use language that suggests powerlessness or a lack of confidence. For example, be aware of allowing interruptions. Stop saying —I'm sorry frequently. Stop the —up talk, that rising inflection at the end of a statement that makes you sound tentative. Become aware of weak language such as tag lines (—this is a good idea, isn't it?), and modifiers (like —hopefully, and —I guess this is a good idea, or even —I'm just the front desk person, or —I'm only a beginner). Our language teaches people how to treat us. If our language lacks power, we are perceived as lacking power and we are treated as lacking power.

Personal power is about our sense of being capable, being confident in the world. It's the belief that we can solve the problems life presents, and conviction in our own ability to succeed. Personal power is important because it unleashes our ability to convey our ideas and solutions in an assured manner. It gives us and others confidence in our ability to solve problems and achieve results. There's nothing like success for boosting our self-confidence, so take some time now to identify your successes. Give yourself permission to take pride in them, and make a sincere effort to recapture and re-experience the emotions you felt when you had your successes.

Grab your smartphone or jump on your tablet, scan the QR code below, and watch this video right now. When finished, spend some time and meditate over what you just read and watched. Ask yourself:

- What will I Apply?

_____
_____
_____
_____
_____
_____

- What will I Change?

_____
_____
_____
_____
_____

- What will I Teach?

# PHASE II

# CHOOSE Your Self:

# Your Story

## PROCESS YOU to SUCCESS

*"If you don't change your beliefs, your life will be like this forever.
Is that good news?*

*-W. Somerset Maugham*

We all have stories—narratives we tell ourselves about why we can or cannot do or achieve something in our lives. Whether we believe we can or can't, we're usually right, because our expectation controls our focus, perceptions, and the way in which we feel and act. When a person succeeds it's because they have the right strategy, and they found it usually because they have a story that it was possible or they could make it happen. Often people are not losing weight because they have a simple story that says, "I'm big boned." With that as your core belief system you are never going to find a strategy, and even if you do you won't follow through on it.

Your story may be true—you may have been through a horrific experience–but that's not the reason why you can't have the life you want. For example, you might have had a bad breakup five years ago, but that's not the reason you haven't found the passionate and loving relationship you deserve. A disempowering story is one of the things that controls people and makes them stuck in their beliefs.

Most people tell a story in a selective way so they don't have to ever maximize their effort towards a strategy because they're afraid they will fail. In order to get out of a story you have to be triggered by hunger and desire—if someone wants something strong enough they will break through the story that's limiting them.

The "story" is the private and public conversation of justifications, reasons, explanations and fixed positions that stand in the way of getting results. We often trade our "story" for the results we intend. We accept our "story" as though it were true, valid and reasonable. We are blind to the fact that we are using our story and selling it to others. This week pay special attention to the "story" that is holding you back or keeping you stuck, stop telling the story; or create a new story that will inspire you and others.

We have the power to "CHOOSE" who we want to be. Once we become Self-Aware of our emotions, our story, and our belief system, we can choose to believe them or choose to create better ones.

*"Between stimulus and response, there is a space. In the space is the power to choose our response. In our response lies our growth and freedom."*

*-Victor Frankl*

# Creating a Better Story

*"Every child is born an artist and the trick of life is to remain an artist."*

*-Picasso*

As a child (and even still today, lol) I was a huge fan of the series Star Trek. The Star Trek theme was "to boldly go where no man has gone before." The crew in Star Trek were on a life-long journey to explore new worlds and uncharted territory in outer space. The space Victor Frankl talks about is inner space. It's not out there in the world. And even though we love stories about journeys to outer space, the journey to inner space is even more rewarding. Every wound, ever negative situation from your past or present, every bad relationship has a message that keeps replaying in the movie of our minds. The wound tells us about us! Crazy right? It's bad enough when others talk about me, but it's another thing when we talk down to ourselves. This put's an imaginary fence around our lives and literally puts "a wall up." This paralyzes you and makes you stuck, watching others live and walk in freedom, the life that our Creator wants us to live. We have to rewrite the script. We have to create a better story. Our God made us so extraordinary and wonderful that we have the choice to choose who we want to be, what we want to be, and the only person that can truly stop us are ourselves! We can't change the past, but what we can do is make new memories. Create better "mind movies" that we replay in our heads. Choose the story you want to live. Choose the legacy that you want left behind. Choose life and let go of anything that doesn't serve your purpose. It will give a liberty that people can't. Repeat after me:

"My old story was fearful, and my new story is mine to create fresh each day. No matter how old I am."

Now we are coaching! That's why coaches such as myself are scorned by those who don't have coaches. This whole issue of changing beliefs and stories while asking for help is a sensitive one to the ego. Coaching and being coachable is a God thing and so is your ego. You can *CHOOSE* to continually "E.dge G.od O.ut" or we can slowly become emotionally fit and "E.xalt G.od O.ver" ever decision we make. If World Class Champions can ask for help and see their life and purpose valuable enough to invest in why can't you? The great runner George Sheehan used to say that we are all athletes, all of us Its just that some of us are in training and some of us are not. That's the big secret that scorners are trying to keep a secret. People change if they are open and willing. If they are willing to let go...

# Let Go of The Weasel!

I once read an interesting story of an eagle that really caught my attention. The Eagle is known as one of the most powerful of all the birds, and is even the symbol of American strength and majesty. In fact, it's even illegal to kill them! In the story, a man noticed an eagle soaring royally through the air, higher and higher, towards great heights. He then observed the eagle swoop down, then quickly begin to ascend to new heights. But then, suddenly without a shot fired, the eagle fell straight to the ground. The man ran curiously towards the eagle to see what happened. He couldn't see anything. As he got closer he noticed two things: The eagle had a weasel in his mouth; and the eagle had a tiny dot of blood close to his heart. Then, out of nowhere, the weasel came out of the eagles mouth and crawled away! Crazy right? The man figured it out. The eagle had came down to eat the weasel. The weasel fighting for his life, pecked recklessly at the eagle. Instead of the eagle letting the small weasel go, he continued to try to soar higher with the weasel pecking away at his heart. Eventually the eagle just dropped dead. Question: How many small, insignificant, past problems, relationships, or issues do you allow to peck away at your heart? Let go. Let go of any belief, perspective, habit, or anything that eat at your heart, so that you can fly to new heights.

Challenge: Repurpose your problems. Re-write your story. Start with the end in mind: What do you want your obituary to say?

Exercise: Throughout this day, begin to explore changing time frames. Whenever you're feeling the pressures of the present, stop and think about the future in ways that are empowering. For example, think of results that compel you, and become fully associated to them. Visualize the image, listen to it, step into it and notice how it feels. Put yourself back into the midst of a treasured memory: your first kiss, the birth of change time frames, the greater your level of freedom and the range of emotions you will be able to create within your at a moment's notice. Do this enough until you truly know you can this change in focus to instantly change your state. Make Sure that you Journal!

# The Power of Creativity

What I've discovered through the value of having my own coaches, mentors and putting myself through various seminars and workshops that put me back on track to having a good life, was that our lives can be the subject matter of creativity. What have to make each day our masterpiece, with our lives being the canvas. We can allow ourselves to apply the creativity that all children have-intuitively, innately-and open it back up and have our financial life creatively invented (constructed) and our physical life be that way too.

Creativity with physical exercise, creativity with finance, creativity even with how you raise children! It's all possible. You can even be creative with how you create relationships in life versus the opposite of that-a life of fear. Without *creating* my relationships I'm just afraid I won't have enough love and approval. So I'll be making all my moves based on my own fears instead of what I want to create. You are an artist and your life is the canvas. Make your life a masterpiece. You are God's masterpiece and you are created to do great work. Believe it and operate like it! Wake up and ask yourself, "What do I want to create today?" Or you can do what's most common, and that is wake up and ask yourself, "What do I fear? What do I dread? What do I hope doesn't happen? What can I avoid? What steps can I take to avoid what I dread the most? And sadly that's how most people live-a full day of avoidance, trying to get around things, trying to avoid something happening-"I hope this audit doesn't happen, I hope she doesn't find out that I'm doing this, and I hope my daughter doesn't think that if I don't send her this money"-and everything is hoping that something doesn't happen; because we are using our creative imagination in the most negative, perverse way because we are using it to worry about the imaginary negative future. Steve Chandler taught me that.

The antidote to that is to reconnect to our power of creativity. If you look at kid , they are running around making up names and making up games all day. They have no identity system to maintain. Therefore they are very creative.

Creative problem solving is a beautiful process. Most people never test it. They never find that out. Because when their problem shows up they just shut down. Instead of going into a quiet tantrum, try asking,

"How can I get creative about this? How can I open my mind? What else is possible? What are some funny, out-of-the-box things that I'm going to try just to play, just to keep people guessing?"

I call this aggressive playfulness. Aggressively pursue life. Give yourself permission to play. Remember that FEAR is only false Evidence Appearing Real. What is real, is what you create. Repurpose your problems. Make them work for your work. Inside each problem or seeming obstacle is the  equal potential for a solution that could possibly be a game changer. You can *choose* to create a better story, and make your fear and your pain your employee. Make them work for your good.

Perspective is everything.

Quit attaching regret to a rough time in your life. Regret can last a lifetime and cripple you emotionally on a consistent basis. The good news is that regret is optional. It's all about your perspective. You can *choose* to "not regret." As John Maxwell says, "Sometimes you win,

Sometimes you learn." Look at every potentially negative story in your life, and find and see a create way that you can repurpose it and learn from it.

# Behavioral Self Control: keeping disruptive emotions and impulses in check

"As human beings, our greatness lie not so much in being able to remake the world... as in being able to remake ourselves." - Mahatma Gandhi

People with this skill

- Manage their impulsive feelings and distressing emotions well

- Stay composed, positive, and unflappable even in trying moments

- Restrain negative reactions

- Think clearly and stay focused under pressure

- Maintain their stamina and performance in emotionally-charged situations

- Choose not to escalate a problem when attacked, provoked, or aggressively confronted by another

- When faced with hostility or opposition, remain —cool under pressure‖

People lacking this skill

- React impulsively

- Get involved in inappropriate situations because they can't resist the temptation

- Respond to problems in a non-constructive way

- Are quick to anger

- Tend to be defensive

May become angry, depressed or agitated when faced with conflicts and stress on the job (may even think of quitting)


"You can't change anything by fighting or resisting it. You change something by making it obsolete through superior methods."

-Buckminster Fuller


As human beings, we operate daily reflecting a wide range of emotions with a multitude of motivations fueling our behaviors. All to often, we react emotionally to what others say or do. If our reactions are preceded by the emotions of fear, anger, or sadness, we forfeit our ability to act with personal power and effectiveness in lieu of a knee-jerk response. This reaction is all to often sourced in fear and low self-esteem. We may focus on what's wrong with us and our lives or fear of being controlled, hurt, or taken advantage of. We may overlook the many things we have in our lives for which we should rightly be grateful. When we doubt our ability to thrive and access the abundance we see all around us in the world, we react instead from the concern of scarcity and the expectation of failure, hurt, and disappointment. We may see ourselves in competition for the world's resources and the love and attention of others rather than realizing that there is more than enough of all that is good to go around. We forget that we manifest what we expect rather than needing to compete for limited resources. I too often produced the fear of not having enough. It showed through my relationships, my reactions, and my thought processes. I was Jemiah's own worst enemy, and my sparatic, paranoid, sometimes "jerkish" behavior showed it.

Whenever we forget that we are magnificent beings made in the image and shadow of a living God and that there is plenty of wealth, happiness, fun, and fulfillment to go around, we might feel the need to protect ourselves from what we perceive to be a dangerous world. The Bible calls this "operating in iniquities," or operating "out of suspicions." This makes it hard for us to form and sustain healthy relationships, and makes us suspicious of the one's that we are already in. Then comes the jealousy, insecurities, paranoia that can even lead to acts of violence rather than be verbal abuse, emotional abuse, and physical abuse-which are all considered domestic violence.

We likewise tend to forget that others operate from the same lacking self-confidence, scarcity of gratitude, and deficient self-love that we often do. So, whenever two or more individuals see themselves as not good enough to tap into the wealth that's already prepared for them, and get all their needs met from a physical, social, mental, and emotional perspective, conflicts are likely to arise. The result is broken relationships, strained communication, emotional pain, struggle, and suffering. All of these are needless and optional for those who realize their ability to detach from the struggle and master their emotional response.

We are to become "responders" rather than "reactors." When we stop to realize that everyone else suffers from the same self-doubt and fear of being dominated and cheated out of getting their fair share of love, fun, money, possessions, and security, we can break the vicious cycle of endless competition and continual striving for domination. We can realize that cooperation and communication is more effective in producing peace than competition and a focus on self-interest based on fear. We can intentionally choose to trust that others are doing the best they know how to do based upon how they see the world. We can assume that they act from good intentions, even when we fear the opposite. We can hold them as worthy, competent, loving, good natured and capable of creating win-win relationships rather than fearing them as hateful, ill meaning, incompetent, unworthy, selfish opponents.

When we decide to champion others by looking for the best in them and interact with them out of an attitude of gratitude for their gifts, strengths, and positive qualities, in such a manner that is clear that we hold them as intrinsically good and worthy of our love and respect, we provide for them a new and exciting opportunity for them to show up for us in the same manner. This is truly managing one's self and being the master of our behavior and relationships. We don't attract good relationships, we create them!

Our decision to hold others as great (because they really are when we strip away their anger, fears, and insecurities) allows them the freedom to rise to our expectations. This also allows us to express or pinned up emotions rather than wait until they explode in a violent (whether verbal or physical) emotionally unfit way. By operating from love and gratitude for the wisdom and "empathy" (we will go more into depth on empathy in future chapters) we develop as a result of our interactions with others, we see their mistakes as temporary indiscretions producing valuable lessons from which to learn and grow rather than reflections of a fundamentally defective being. This is emotion fitness and social responsibility at its finest and an example of making anger your employee! Use that energy and make it work for you!

The key to bringing out the best in others is non-attachment. When we realize that we have total control over our response to any situation, and we give up our right to be invalidated by others or control them, we will possess a newfound freedom that allows us to exit the drama of conflict in favor of understanding, compassion, and love. This is self-love and an expression of self-compassion. This freedom helps to free us from the burden of frustration when others don't meet our "unspoken" expectations. This makes us emotionally fit enough to make clear, major decisions based on truth rather than decisions based off of the reactions and the false assumptions of others.

Action Step: Decide now to be grateful for the challenges you will encounter in your life, career, and business. See the problems that arise as opportunities for your personal development. Look for these challenges as you go about your day, be grateful when you encounter them, and seek out the gifts awaiting your discovery.

Exercise for Expanding Gratitude and Shifting Your Reactive Nature

- List all the things you have decided to be grateful for in your life, career, relationships, or business.

- In your daily journal, record each time you fail to express gratitude for a challenging situation.

- Catch yourself reacting emotionally to what someone says or does and shift your perception in the moment to appreciate the learning experience at hand.

- In your daily life, career, relationships, and business, who are you not holding as significant & highly esteemed?

- How can you champion their excellence and express gratitude for the opportunity o grow in love and wisdom that they are gifting you instead of reacting with anger, sadness, or fear?

- Who are you seeking to control or avoid being controlled by?

Challenge: Will you take on the practice of non-attachment in your relationship with them by creating space for them to be who they are? Do this for 30 days and record in your journal how your interactions with them evolve. Make note of something that you can be grateful for each situation.


Development tips

- Self awareness is the first step
- Make a list of things that cause you to —lose it‖ – your triggers or —hot buttons‖
- Write out a strategy to deal with each of these issues the next time they arise
- Remember, in the moment, to choose a more constructive response when issues come up in the future
- Watch yourself talk – tell yourself what it looks like to stay composed, stay focused & think clearly under pressure
- When having "pity parties," shift back in the present moment and ask, "How can I make a difference?"

Grab your smartphone or jump on your tablet, scan the QR code below, and watch this video right now. When finished, spend some time and meditate over what you just read and watched. Ask yourself:

- What will I Apply?

  _____

  _____

  _____

  _____

  _____

- What will I Change?

  _____

  _____

  _____

  _____

  _____

- What will I Teach?

  _____

  _____

  _____

  _____

  _____

PROCESS YOU to SUCCESS

# Phase III

# GIVE Your Self:

# Your Strategy

# Give

A lot of times in life, even when we know our self, and choose the story that we want to tell, we often still get stuck right there. We get worried about not coming across as cocky, not coming across as arrogant, not coming across as too confident. I'm going to give you some advice that I had to drill into my own head and that one of my coaches had to tell me: Stop coming across. Start making a difference. GIVE yourself. We have a feeling in our own gut that there is something more than life that we are missing. We all long for fire and passion to fill our lives. We ache to grasp and fulfill our heart's desires. We crave a destiny of our own. In short, we want to be alive.

Question: What do you feel you are missing in your life and how are you going to find it? Do you want to die before learning what it means to be truly alive, to feel passion and wonder and excitement once again?

People are incredibly obsessed throughout the day with how they are coming across, how to say this, how to do that. That's the one problem I have with all of this "attraction" thing. Attraction shouldn't be a goal. Creating the results I want to see should. When we are trying to "attract" it is almost as if we are trying to manipulate other people's love and approval. It never works. Authenticity does. Attraction normally backfires. The more obsessed with how you are coming across, the more repulsed other people are my phony attempts to impress. Just be you and let your real crowd of supporters show. Give yourself. Make a difference. Instead of asking,

"How am I coming across?" ask "How can I make a difference? How can I contribute? How can I help? This takes this focus off of you. Whenever you value difference-making in your world, your world literally becomes different. You seem start living a life of "creating" relationships, creating value, creating money, creating results, and creating what you want versus trying to attract it. Trying to attract friends and wealth from outside of you solidifies your self-concept as deficient, defective, and not enough. You want to shift to being your whole self. An emotionally fit and socially responsible self. Giving is living. Find your purpose, then give it to the world. There is a famous quote by George Bernard Shaw on the subject of living on purpose. When you read this quote, compare it to being lost. Because the longer I live the more I realize that life is a choice between this quote by Shaw…and being lost. The quote says:

"This is the true joy in life, the being used for a purpose recognized by yourself as a mighty one; to being a force of nature instead of a feverish selfish little cold of ailments and grievances complaining that the world will not devote itself to making you happy.

I am of the opinion that my life belongs to the whole community, and as long as I live it is my privilege to do for it whatever I can.

I want to be thoroughly used up when I die, for the harder I work the more I live. I rejoice in life for its own sake. Life is no 'brief candle' for me. It is a sort of splendid torch which I have got hold of for the moment, and I want to make it burn as brightly as possible before handing it on to future generations."

Be authentic. Know you...Choose you...then give the best you to your world.

# Empathy: The Bridge

*"We are, each of us, angels with only one wing; and we can only fly embracing each other."*

-*Luciano de Crescenzo*

"Seek first to understand, before seeking to be understood..."- Steven Covey

"People want to know that you care, more than they care what you know." If you don't know the values and rules of the people with whom you share a relationship, you should prepare for pain. People can love each other, but if for whatever reason they consistently break the rules of someone they care about, there are going to be upsets and stress in this relationship. I once heard this story of a blind man: An old man with dark glasses was sitting on a busy street corner during rush hour. He was playing a saxophone and begging for money. On the cardboard sign, next to an empty tin cup, he had written: 'Blind – Please Help.' Despite the sign, no one was stopping and giving him any money. After a while, a young advertising writer walked past and saw the blind man with his sign and empty cup, and also saw that many people were passing by completely unmoved, let alone stopping to give him money. The advertising writer took a thick marker from his pocket, turned the sheet of cardboard over and rewrote the sign, and then went on his way. Immediately, people began putting money into the tin cup. After a while, when the cup was overflowing with coins and dollar bills, the blind man asked a stranger to tell him what the sign now said. "It says," said the stranger, "It's a beautiful day. You can see it. I cannot."

86

PROCESS YOU to SUCCESS

# Developing Empathy

*"If there is any great secret of success in life, it lies in the ability to put yourself in the other person's place and to see things from his point of view – as well as your own."*

*– Henry Ford*

## What Is Empathy?

The Greater Good Science center at Yale University states that the term "empathy" is used to describe a wide range of experiences. Emotion researchers generally define empathy as the ability to sense other people's emotions, coupled with the ability to imagine what someone else might be thinking or feeling. Contemporary researchers often differentiate between two types of empathy: "Affective empathy" refers to the sensations and feelings we get in response to others' emotions; this can include mirroring what that person is feeling, or just feeling stressed when we detect another's fear or anxiety. "Cognitive empathy," sometimes called "perspective taking," refers to our ability to identify and understand other people's emotions. Studies suggest that people with autism spectrum disorders have a hard time empathizing. Empathy seems to have deep roots in our brains and bodies, and in our evolutionary history. Elementary forms of empathy have been observed in our primate relatives, in dogs, and even in rats. Empathy has been associated with two different pathways in the brain, and scientists have speculated that some aspects of empathy can be traced to mirror neurons, cells in the brain that fire when we observe someone else perform an action in much the same way that they would fire if we performed that action ourselves. Research has also uncovered evidence of a genetic basis to empathy, though studies suggest that people can enhance (or restrict) their natural empathic abilities. Having empathy doesn't necessarily mean we'll want to help someone in need, though it's often a vital first step toward compassionate action.

Empathy is defined as  sensing others' feelings and perspectives, and taking an active interest in their concerns; the ability to put yourself in another's place and to take that perspective into account in your relationship with the other person.

People with this competence

- Are attentive to and able to attune to a wide range of emotional signals

- Listen for and sense the felt, but unspoken emotions in a person or group

- Show sensitivity to and understand others' perspectives and feelings – they can —walk a mile in the other persons moccasins‖

- Are able to help the other person or the group based on an accurate understanding of their needs and feelings

People lacking this competence

- Stereotype others

- Show no understanding, or misunderstand, or are surprised by others' feelings or actions

- Often come into conflict

- Don't attempt to understand people and what they are thinking and feeling.

- Tend to act without considering how others might feel about something

- Come across as indifferent or uncaring

Development tips

- Listening is the key to empathy. Quiet your mind, still the inner clamor, and listen deeply for more than the other person's words. Listen for the other person's needs (i.e., to be respected, to be included, to be acknowledged?)

- Identify underlying concerns that are not explicitly stated by others

- Hear the emotions that accompany an expressed statement

- Listen when someone approaches you to express their feelings (don't be so busy you can't talk with the other person about what's important to them; don't brush them off)

# Empathetic Maturity, Love, & Relationships

In 2001, a Dr. Olson wrote about three stages of Empathetic Maturity. Google his work if you're a reader, it's quite interesting. I'm going to share them, then elaborate on the discussion.

Stage 1 – This most primitive pattern and not common in adults. Persons at this stage see others as fundamentally different from themselves. The rationale for another's actions, feelings, or thoughts are not experienced as having human relevance in the sense that one's own rationale do. Those operating at this stage perceive mutuality with others concretely.

Stage 2 – People at Stage 2 hold that their own rationale for behavior is valid for everyone. Therefore, reasons for behaviors and feelings are legitimate only to the degree they coincide with the person at Stage 2. Unlike Stage 1, the Stage 2 person sees others like him or her so long as make sense of their world the same way. Therefore, positive regard for a sufferer perceived to be participating in negative behaviors is difficult for the Stage 2 person unless the behavior is explicable from his or her point of view. An example of such negative behavior would be AIDS as the result of sex practices not condoned by the Stage 2 observer. If the Stage 2 person believes the sufferer is responsible for the behavior, he or she will have no empathy. If the Stage 2 person can detect an acceptable reason why the sufferer is not actually responsible, for example, illness resulted from blood transfusion, beyond the sufferer's control, then empathy emerges. Whether empathy and compassion occurs depends on the individual's value judgments and understanding of what caused the suffering. Most of society operates at Stage 2.

Stage 3 – At this stage, empathy occurs prior to and without regard for any judgment about the person's behavior. The other is perceived as human in the same way the self is experienced as human. The perception of another person as responsible for a problem no longer has the power to hinder the development of empathy. If the sufferer is seen as responsible, there is no longer any need to mitigate that responsibility as a method for allowing empathy. A hallmark of Stage 3 is a person's ability to perceive another empathetically while simultaneously and without apparent contradiction perceiving that other as responsible for problematic behavior.

I found Dr. Olson's findings very interesting. I've come to understand that the ability to empathize is dependent first on our abilities to feel and identify our own feelings and emotions. If we are to coach our clients in the skills of empathy, they must first have mastered the ability to know, understand and name their own emotions. If we are not aware that we have experienced a certain feeling, it is difficult for us to understand what another person is feeling. A prerequisite to coaching empathy is coaching emotional self-awareness.


From the standpoint of emotional intelligence, empathy involves at least three concepts:

1. Listening for another's emotional state and having a sensitivity for the other person's feelings, is arguably the first step

2. Understanding what that person might be feeling or

experiencing at this moment, both cognitively and emotionally, and

3.  Verbally expressing, communicating and acknowledging our perception of the —internal frame of reference of another‖ and our —sense of similarity of feelings.

Empathy is the capacity to know – emotionally – what another is experiencing, AND being able to express or communicate our feelings of empathy. If we do not, we may feel empathy, but the other person may not know that we do. To enhance the relationship, it is important to express (verbally, or through our body language, tone, or actions) that we understand, acknowledge and share the experience and feelings of the other person. When people feel listened to and understood at a deep emotional level, and when that is acknowledged or communicated, people feel affirmed and validated. Empathy is a core competency of being emotionally fit.

Remember, every upset you've ever had with another human being has been a rules upset, and when people become intimately involved, it's inevitable that some of their rules will clash. By knowing a person's rules, you can head off these challenges in advance Communicate to Connect, not just to hear yourself talk. Relationships have to be based on Love & respect. In John Maxwell's book "How to be a R.E.A.L. Success," the "R", standing for relationships, is my favorite. Success is worthless if we don't have someone to share it with. Our most desired human emotion is that of connection with other souls (Think why God create Eve. It is not good for man to be alone. When people say, "All I need is Jesus", they're emotionally wounded from a relationship. Throughout this book we've talked consistently about the impact of relationships on shaping character, values, belief systems, and the quality of our lives Take the time today to talk with your significant other and find out what's most important to each of you in your relationship.

Challenge: What are your highest values in a relationship together, and what has to happen for you to feel like those values are being fulfilled?

Exercise:

- Decide that it's more important for you to be in love than to be right. If you should ever find yourself in the position of insisting that you're right, break your own pattern. Stop immediately and come back to the discussion later when you're in a better state to resolve your conflicts. Tony Robbins once said to "make your relationships one of the highest priorities in your life; otherwise they will take a back seat to any or all of the other things that are more urgent that happen during your day." Gradually, the level of emotional intensity and passion will drift away.

We don't want to lose the power of our relationships simply because we got caught up in the law of familiarity, or we let neglect habituate us to the intense excitement and passion we have for a person.

Social and Emotional Fitness does not exist apart from relationships. We are created, developed, and sustained in relationship throughout our lives. Our brain and our emotional fitness develop in relationship. As adults, our emotional fitness is dynamic. Most of us go up and down with our emotional fitness depending upon the situation and the stress we are under

# Understanding Your "Why"

Your Why comes from Your Hurt, Your Heart, and Your Help. These are the 3 ways that people will connect with you.

### Your Hurt:

Your hurt is your pain, your past, those experiences that give you the fuel to keep going. Your "why" is rooted in the things that disgust you the most; the things that you have personally lived through. I have personally been emotionally obese and socially unfit. I know how it feels to be in a bad, unhealthy relationship. I know how it feels to appear successful on the outside and on your bank statement, but are emotionally & relationally bankrupt on the inside.

### Your Heart:

Your heart is based from your pain. Your heart is what you care about. Those things and causes that you want to make a difference and impact in. I choose to only work with people that want to make an impact on the lives of others. I truly believe that if your vision came from above that it will, and must include developing and empowering others. If someone doesn't know their vision, it's my purpose to help them pull it out. Your heart is your concerns, your passion that burns deep within.

### Your Help:

Your help is what you want to offer, your solutions. The goal is to not just become a role model. Those are replaceable. The goal is to become a resource that is invaluable. I truly believe that God placed a piece of eternity in each of us that is priceless and immeasurable. That, .y friend, is what you offer the world.

Exercise: Based on the definitions above, defined you "Why":

My Hurt

_____

_____

_____

_____

_____

_____

My Heart:

_____

_____

_____

_____

_____

_____

My Help:

_____

_____

_____

_____

_____

Your "why" is intertwined with your Vision. Your "Why" actually births your vision.

A vision shows up on the inside to show you what's possible on the outside. You can (and should) have a vision for your family, yourself, your relationships, your business and career, your spiritual growth and development, and your health. Bringing your vision from your mind to reality will take work and consistency. But count the costs. The Vision has its own set time to manifest. The value is in the preparation and the process. Don't sweat the small stuff that happens along the way. There will be discouraging times when it looks like nothing is happening or that your vision isn't even in sight. Keep moving towards it until you can see it clearly. It's all about perspective. You will hear me say this a lot. Perspective is always key. Ask yourself, "do I cry over spilled milk? Or do I just clean it up and keep moving, knowing that I could get some more, or that maybe that carton was spoiled anyway? Perspective can and will be the difference maker and momentum keeper. Your perspective has to have a focal point, and that focal point is your vision. Can you stay big picture focused when storms come? When unfortunate situations occur? When circumstances happen that are out of your control?

A vision gives purpose to actions and helps make decisions when you reach those forks in the road. And trust me, you will reach several forks in the road. Stay the course. You don't have to react to everything, but do have to respond, even if that response is the decision to be silent. What are you holding on to that is keeping you from truly immersing yourself in your vision and purpose? Is it an identity? Is it a reputation? Is it pride? Is it the past? How is what you're holding on to helping you live out your purpose and make

your greatest impact on this side of the ground?
Please...Please...Live!

# Achievement Drive & Getting Results!

"Life is no brief candle for me. It is a sort of splendid torch which I have got hold of for the moment, and I want to make it burn as brightly as possible before handing it on to future generations."

- George Bernard Shaw

People with this skill

- Are results-oriented, with a high drive to meet their objectives and standards

- Set —stretch goals‖ -- challenging yet reachable

- Take moderate, calculated risks

- Pursue information to reduce uncertainty and find ways to do better

- Learn how to improve their performance

People lacking this competence

- Tend to avoid firm, fixed standards of performance, whether actively and overtly or passively and covertly

- Work without regard to expectations and do not push themselves

- Often do the minimum to get by

- Don't take goals seriously, and if pressed to make them, set easy goals they can effortlessly attain or impossible goals they fail to meet (so they can say —I told you so‖)

- Accept the status quo, don't —rock the boat‖

- Do what's required of them and no more

- May get the work done when goals are set for them, but don't demonstrate an interest in working independently to an internal standard of excellence

Achievement drive is defined as having high personal and professional standards, and striving to improve or meet new, higher standards of excellence; continuously learning. Achievement drive is needed to become emotionally fit and to accomplish what you set out to do. To help improve your achievement drive you need to define the results you want to achieve and execute the goals you need to bring them into reality.

## Goal Setting vs. Results

Achieving a goal is like opening a combination lock. You need the correct numbers in the correct right, left, right sequence. There are thousands of possible combinations and if you're aware of the setting but not the sequence, your efforts will just frustrate and discourage you. That's why I recommend setting your results first, then set your goals to achieve the results.

Create routines, not commitments. When we say things like, "I want to lose 50 pounds," that's a commitment. When we say, "I will spend 20 min a day on the treadmill," we are creating a routine that will get us our desired results. We spoke a little on this earlier in the book. When we create only commitments and things don't work like we want them to we complicate them and add stories to them, in ex: "I'm not good at this…I'm bad at that..I guess this must not be for me…etc, etc." This makes it harder to change and make a difference in our lives and the lives of others. This is self-condemnation in one of it's most subtle forms. Succeeding is much easier than it looks. Instead of making commitments, we can create habits and routine that ultimately get us to our desired results. Commitments are defaults of what you actually. What you do shows your commitment. Makes sense?

Development Tips

- Set results first, before goals, and standards of excellence to accomplish them. NEVER set goals first. Goals are negotiable, results are not. Results are measurable. Goals can give a false sense of accomplishment if they are the initial and main focus point.

- Get in touch with the emotional pull of what you want to achieve and why – what do you gain by going the extra mile? What do you lose by not taking action or going for more?

- Keep a daily log of your achievements

- Take at least one step each day toward your goals

- Establish moderate risks for achieving your goals

- Make your goals —SMART‖ – specific, measurable, achievable, realistic and timed;

PROCESS YOU to SUCCESS

# Resilience

Resilience is defined as having perseverance and diligence in the face of setbacks

<u>People with this competence</u>

- Know how to cope in spite of setbacks, barriers or limited resources

- Are willing and able to overcome obstacles to get what they want

- Bounce back from adversity and disappointments

- Are flexible and adaptable

- See setbacks as temporary and failures as isolated and short term

<u>People lacking this competency</u>

- See failure as permanent

- Demonstrate inflexible thinking

- Tend to dwell in the past, get —stuck in the past and can't move forward

- Experience a great deal of negative —self-talk (—what were you thinking? or —you'll never come back from this one)

Development tips

- For starters, practice healthy living – we can't be resilient if we're lacking sleep, are stressed, or mal-nourished.

- Build in periods of rest and renewal so you can face life's inevitable tough times with strength

- Challenge the negative —self-talk – ask yourself, —what's my real belief here? and —is there any evidence behind this self-doubt?

- See setbacks as temporary and disappointments as isolated, short term and specific to the circumstance, not as permanent or applicable to all situations

- Seek support from others in your life – encircle yourself with helpful family and friends –you don't have to go it alone

- Read biographies of resilient people and learn from them

# Focus!

Where focus goes, energy flows. And where energy flows, whatever you're focusing on grows. In other words, your life is controlled by what you focus on. That's why you need to focus on where you want to go, not on what you fear. When you next find yourself in a state of uncertainty, resist your fear. Shift your focus toward where you want to go and your actions will take you in that direction. Focus on your "Why" and your "Vision." Align your emotions and your whole state of being with your why and your vision. Success is not a destination, but a direction: Forward. You don't have to kick a hole in the universe to be successful, but rather, take progressive steps daily.

Congratulations my friend, you are well on your way to becoming emotionally fit and creating breakthrough in any area of your life!!!

# Contribution

*"The secret to living is giving"*

*-Tony Robbins.*

Being a "Servant Leader" sets you apart in your family, your career, and in anything you put your hand to. This is a crucial part of becoming emotionally fit and socially responsible.. (Give example of Robert Greenleaf and the 10 principles of Servant Leadership). So many people feel powerless and insignificant when it comes to social issues and world events, thinking that even if they did everything right in their own personal lives, their welfare would still be at the mercy of the actions of others. They feel beset by the proliferation of gang warfare and violent crime, perplexed by massive government deficits, massive unemployment, saddened by homelessness and illiteracy, and overwhelmed by global warming and the relentless extinction of the other species that live on this planet. Such people fall into the mindset of thinking, "Even if I get my own life and the lives of my family in order, what good will it do? Some nut in a position of power could accidentally push the button and blow us all up anyway!" This kind of belief system fosters the feeling of being out of control and impotent to create change at any significant level, and naturally leads to the learned helplessness typified by the phrase, "Why even try?" Nothing could be more crippling to a person's ability to take action than learned helplessness; it is the primary obstacle that prevents us from changing our lives or taking action to help other people change theirs. If you've come this far in the book, you know without a doubt my central message: you have the power right now to control how you think, how you feel, and what you do.

Perhaps for the first time you are empowered to take control of the Master System that has unconsciously guided you until this point. With the strategies and distinctions you've gained from reading and doing the exercises in this book, you have awakened to the conviction that you are truly the master of your fate, the director of your destiny. Together we've discovered the giant power that shapes destiny—Decision and Choice shapes destiny. our decisions about what to focus on, what things mean, and what to do are the decisions that will determine the quality of our present and future. Your Power is your ability to Choose. Nobody, No devil can ever take that away. You can lose money, homes, businesses, but you never lose ability to choose. You can always make a difference. You contribute to this world by simply CHOOSING to be YOU. Being YOU is where your highest value is because there is none other like you. This makes you a rare commodity. This makes you a "precious gem." When you fully BE the person that God created you to be, you are truly giving the World your highest value! Make sense? It's only one *(insert your name here)!* *Be YOU! Your ability to deal with your own challenges becomes a minor focus. What used to be difficult becomes easy. At this point, you'll find yourself redirecting your energies from concentrating primarily on yourself to improving what's happening in your family, your community, and possibly the world around you. The only way to do so with a lasting sense of fulfillment is through unselfish contribution—because the secret to living is giving. So don't look for heroes; be one! Here are some of the ways you can help. A small amount of time can make a big difference. Consider the possibility of committing a few hours a week or a few hours a month in one of the following areas within your community outlined by one of my mentors from afar, Tony Robbins (Citate "Awaken the Giant Within")*

   *- Your Church (If you don't belong to one, find one!)*

   *-Programs for the mentally and physically disabled*

   *- Voter registration*

   *- Energy conservation*

- *Park maintenance*

- *Volunteer for a local non-profit*

- *Emergency aid*

- *Volunteering at a local soup kitchen*


Teach others that their value and opportunity is inside of them, and to use hard times as motivation to find it. This is exercising true compassion. Compassion is one's aspiration that people don't suffer, but grow daily. Don't just add value, but multiply! Love fixes everything! The beautiful thing about love is that it is contagious. Do you measure your success by the success of the people connected to you, or by the things you just do for yourself? The seeds of love and compassion yields immeasurable fruit and results that can leave a legacy that will last years after you are gone. Listen more. Listen without power. This empowers the person or people around you to actually strive to do more! When you show empathy, you empower the people in your relationship to move forward. Can you listen in a powerless way? Try it for 30 days. I promise that it will change the quality of your relationships and the quality of your life.


*Whatever you are thinking of doing, picture yourself at 90, and how you would feel if you didn't try. On their deathbeds, people never ask for more money or more possessions. You never hear anyone dying say. "Man...if I could only make $50 more bucks!" The thing that most people ask for and ask for is more time. Value you time and at least try. You owe to your family. You owe to the world. You owe it to your creator. You owe it to yourself.*

*Now it's time to Jump!*

"COME TO THE EDGE, " HE SAID.
THEY SAID,"WE ARE AFRAID."
"COME TO THE EDGE." HE SAID.
THEY CAME.
HE PUSHED THEM.
AND THEY FLEW…
- GUILLAUME APOLLINAIRE

"The winner of a race is not the fastest person in the race, but the person who gets started first. Get…Started!"

Grab your smartphone or jump on your tablet, scan the QR code below, and watch this video right now. When finished, spend some time and meditate over what you just read and watched. Ask yourself:

- What will I Apply?

  _____
  _____
  _____
  _____
  _____
  _____

- What will I Change?

  _____
  _____
  _____

_____

_____

_____

● What will I Teach?

_____

_____

_____

_____

_____

_____

# Process Y.O.U.: The World is Yours!

*"For God so Loved the World...."*

*-The Apostle John*

*"You have to be burning with an idea, or a problem, or a wrong that you want to right. If you're not passionate enough to start, you will never be passionate enough to stick it out."*

*—Steve Jobs*

It's a verse in the Bible that I absolutely love. I'm pretty sure you've heard, even if you're not a Christian. It's found in the book of John, Chapter three, verse sixteen, and it reads,

"For God so Loved the World so much that He sent His only Son, so that He that believes in Him may not perish, but, have everlasting life."

That verse ignites something in me. The word "World" used in that verse is translate into the Greek word "cosmos". The definition and Greek root word means " system of things", "process." "order""For God so loved His order", His Process. Say Yes to the Process. God is and always will be in the Character Development Business. Develop you from the inside out.

Remember that a tree grows down, before it grows up. The Process serves as your foundation. Process Y.our O.wn U.niverse.

## PROCESS YOU to SUCCESS

All of creation is waiting....

Tony Robbins once said, "Change your strategy, change your result.

Change your story, change your life.

Change your state—you change it all!"

Stay the Course!

To sum all of this up in simplistic terms. Here's 3 ways to help you stay committed to becoming emotionally fit:

1. Solve small problems. This keeps you in the now. Plan for the future, but manage your today. The only time you have control of is the present.
2. Make your bed. Yep..I said it, make your bed. This way you will always have completed at least 1 thing for the day, and you will have accomplished something perfectly, which will get you in the routine of finishing perfectly. One of my mentors, Jonathan Sprinkles, reminded me of a story that Will Smith told.
3. Finish what you start. Period. Keep Going....

I believe in YOU!! There is a whole world designed and waiting for you to show up. To show up Emotionally Fit, mentally tough, and Socially responsible. A world that needs your impact. Cheers to YOU and your next!!!

PROCESS YOU to SUCCESS

# Extra Resources, Encouragement, Personal Notes, and Exercises that have helped me

# Understanding Change

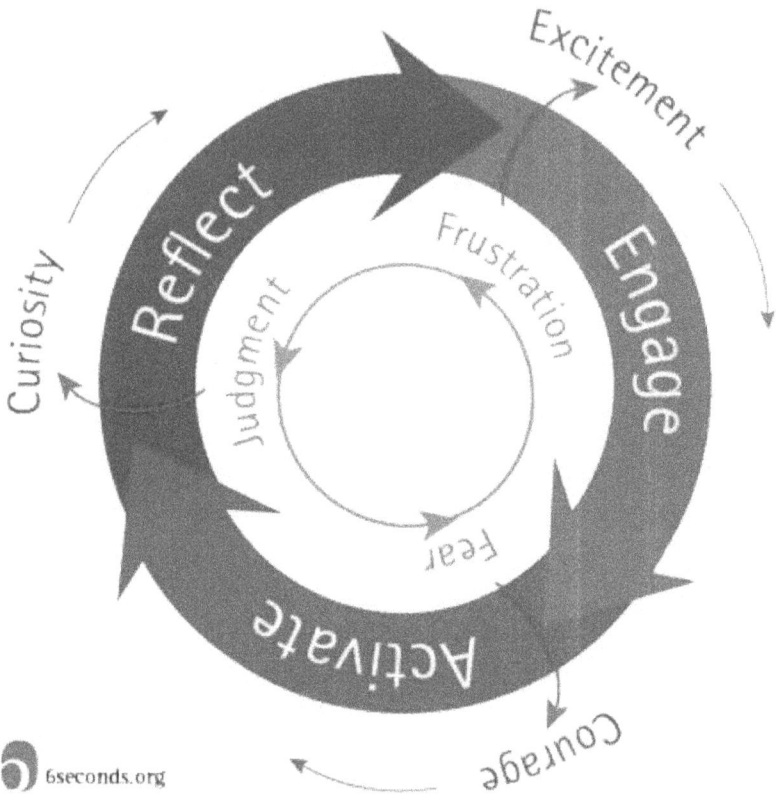

6seconds.org

## Phase 1 – Engage

In the first stage of change the goal is to believe and buy in to your plan and vision. You have to believe in yourself before you expect anyone else.

You have to create a clear, accurate understanding of your current reality from a logical as well as emotional level. This is how you set the results that you want and develop the goals to get you there. This is a very delicate part of the change process.

Most change fails due to lack of engagement of ourselves and of the people and relationships we invite or let into our process of change. At a logical level, it's moving from definition to strategy. At an emotional level it's about people feeling heard, acknowledging the frustration, and building a seed of hope. You first need to begin to feel that change is possible, then the people attached to you.

## Phase 2 – Activate

Based on the awareness and readiness created in phase 1, the next step is to create new successes by generating new knowledge, attitudes, and skills. Typically, this phase requires learning — new insight to see differently, shared vocabulary to communicate about what's driving people, and new skills to build strong, healthy relationships.

In this phase, one of the key challenges is maintaining focus. A "training" is not enough to create change — it takes a process. We recommend a blended-learning approach with assessments, exceptionally powerful learning experiences, and personalized and small-group coaching to go from awareness into action.

In this phase, it's also important to build capacity, on an individual level and with whom you are overall connected to. These principles are the same even if you are creating change in an organization.

In this phase, the goal is to experience success — for people to go into action and to experience for themselves that their change is working.

## Phase 3 – Reflect

"Reflect" is about mining the previous phases. Return to the methods collected, re-measure, identify progress. Examine the results from both logical and emotional lenses. Learn — learning doesn't require success, it requires curiosity. Show what worked and the value of it.

Typically, people think of change as something that is planned then executed, and that's it. In reality, we know that high performing organizations don't just make a change, they become good at change. This phase is key to that transformation because here the person or organization mines the successes and failures of the previous stages and then builds on those for the next round. The goal is to increase forward momentum — and accuracy.

The goal of this phase is to lock-in the wins — to be clear about the successes and failures and then to build on those to propel the change to the next level.

People aren't wrong, systems are. Draw from your future to create a system to get there. This may be uncomfortable, but all change is. If you are experiencing pain, this is just an indication that you need order, and change will help usher that in. Systems are built to maintain an expected end. What is the expected end of your career, your relationships, if you don't get emotionally fit? If you never change your systems or routines? By default we go to self-pity and condemnation: It must be something in my past...The Psychology game..The Past life. Build the future with the future. Create new systems to get new results. This is how your brain works. Once you get this system down pack, it makes it easier to create break-though in any circumstance in your life. Embrace…Embrace…Embrace change.

# Becoming a More Solution Oriented Team Player

How do you look at life? Do you see a solution in every challenge or a problem in every circumstance? To make yourself a more solution-oriented team player....

*Refuse to Give Up.* Thinking about an impossible situation you and your teammates hall all but given up overcoming. Now determine to not give up until you find a solution.

*Refocus your Thinking.* No problem can withstand the assault of sustained thinking. Set aside dedicated time with key teammates to work on the problem. Make sure it's prime think time, not left over time when you're tired or distracted.

*Rethink your Strategy.* Get out of the box of your typical thinking. Break a few rules. Brainstorm absurd ideas. Redefine the problem. Do whatever it takes to generate fresh ideas and approaches to the problem.

*Repeat the Process.* If at first you don't succeed in solving the problem, keep at it. If you do solve the problem, then repeat the process with another problem. Remember, your goal is to create a solution-oriented attitude that you can bring into play all the time.

# PROCESS YOU to SUCCESS

*Do you see a problem in every circumstance or a solution in every challenge?*

# 5 Ingredients of Personal Growth

As any farmer knows, the growth of a crop only happens when the right ingredient are present. To harvest plentiful fields, the farmer has to begin by planting the right seed in rich topsoil where sunlight and water can help the seed to sprout, mature, and bear fruit. If any of the ingredients (seeds, topsoil, sunlight, or water) are missing, the crop won't grow.

Growing as a person also requires the proper ingredients. Unless the right attitudes and actions are cultivated you will sputter and fail rather than growing in influence. Let's look at five basic qualities essential for personal growth.

1. Teachability- Arrogance crowds out room for improvement. That's why humility is the starting point for personal growth. As Erwin G. Hall said, "An open mind is the beginning of self-discovery and growth. We can't learn anything new until we can admit that we don't know everything already." Adopting a beginner's mindset helps you to be teachable. Beginners are aware that they don't know it all, and they proceed accordingly. As a general rule, they're open and humble, noticeably lacking in the rigidity that often accompanies experience and achievement. It's easy enough to have a beginner's mind when you're actually a beginner, but maintaining teachability gets trickier in the long term especially when you think you have already achieved some degree of success.

2.  Sacrifice- Growth as a leader involves temporary loss. It may mean giving up familiar but limiting patterns, safe but unrewarding work, values no longer believed in, or relationships that have lost their meaning. Whatever the case, everything we gain in life comes as a result of sacrificing something else. We must give up to go up.

3.  Security- To keep learning throughout life, you have to be willing, no matter what your position is to say, "I don't know." It can be hard to admit lacking knowledge because you may feel as if everyone is looking to you for direction, and they don't want to let people down, however, most people aren't searching for perfection, they're looking for an honest, authentic, and courageous individuals who, regardless of the obstacles facing them will keep working and won't rest until the situation is solved. One must be secure enough to keep taking the stage and honing your skills until you can connect. Being insecure, listening to negative evaluations of others, will seal your fate and you will not excel.

4.  Listening- Listen, learn, and ask questions from somebody successful who has gone on before you borrow from their experiences so that you can avoid their mistakes and emulate their triumphs. Solicit feedback and take to heart what you're told. The criticism of friends may seem bitter in the short-term but, when heeded, it can save you from falling victim to your blind spots.

5.  Application- Knowledge has a limited shelf life. Unless used immediately or carefully preserved, it spoils and becomes worthless. Put the lessons you learn into practice so that your

insights mature into understanding.

*"It is necessary to try to surpass one always; this occupation ought to last as long as life."*

*-Christina, Queen of Sweden*

# 7 Steps of Letting Go of the Past

1. Let go of the baggage.- Whether we realize or not, as long as we hold on to our past, it serves as a heavy weight on us. We need to let it go! Write the names of the past pains on a sheet of paper and have a ceremonial "burning" to help you get in touch with letting go of the pain forever. Imagine that I tossed you my keys and then walked away. Someone comes to me and says, "I need your keys, Can you give them to me?" I have to explain that I no longer have the keys. In the same way, I "toss my cares" to God...then if someone asks for those cares (my mind or emotions), then I can send them to God who has them!

2. Close that chapter.- "That was then, this is now." Rather than going back and re-reading the chapter over and over again, close that chapter in your life. Move on...read on to your future. You can't read two chapters at the same time. Close that chapter and let it go. Let it get dusty on your life bookshelf.

3. Quit talking about the past.- Every time we talk about the problem or the pain, we take what is in the past and bring it back into our present day! God forgets our past...so should we. An individual did something very unkind to you...a very selfish act with you as the victim. We have the choice to either let it go...and not tell anyone about it. Or, we could call a friend and cry on their shoulder and every time someone would ask about this person, we could go over the recent hurt...Or, we could make a commitment to ourselves and those we love not to talk

about it. When we do this, it allows the pain of this act to leave. This is also important part of forgiving a person. Our motive of telling others would be to bring revenge and hurt...and we all know that's not our job to do!

4.  Let go of the shame.- we make mistakes. Sometimes we consciously or unconsciously do things that hurt ourselves or others or we flat out do things, knowing it's not the Way. Even if we have accepted forgiveness, we must let go of the shame that may try to linger. Instead of dwelling on the shame, focus on the new spirit in you. Be thankful for the fact: "That was then and this is now." You are anew and can shed the shame.

5.  Enjoy today!- We've all read about or listened to teachings about the power of gratitude and positive thinking.! But few of us engage in the practice. Engage is a verb and it requires us to take action. If we are to enjoy the day, we need to do it. I can't learn to enjoy the day for you. You just have to enjoy the day for yourself. You can enjoy it by making a conscious decision to look at the positive things in your life, as small as they may seem right now.

6.  Walk by faith not by sight.- This should be "how we are." To walk by faith you need to "know" Truth, and when you "know" Truth you can "do" truth. You have an inner confidence and conviction that propels you forward regardless if you can see it or not! Make a decision today to walk by what you know to be Truth1

7.  Believe and understand the power of forgiveness.- This is a big one! If you have unforgiveness in your heart, GET RID OF IT! Do you hear me shouting? I realized in my own life the power of

forgiveness. It frees you, whether or not the other person changes or apologizes or not. When something comes up, call it out, and make the steps to forgive in that area. Remember that forgiving and trusting are two different things. Trust is earned. Forgiveness is a free gift, no strings attached. You can forgive a person and still not trust them and that's okay. Forgiveness is not accepting the person's action as right. Just God forgives us, and believe me, He does, we must forgive others. Forgiveness is Divine. No one else can forgive for you. You are the only one who can and must forgive those who have hurt you, done you wrong or caused you damage. I know…it's hard. But, the benefits of forgiveness outweigh the acts. Letting go of the past takes work. If we want to move into a New Beginning, we must let go of the past. Again, the choice is yours. Will you purpose to do it? Or will you stay in the rut of your past?

# "If"

This a very dear poem that was given to me by one of my mentors, a dear friend, a big brother, and my spiritual father, Pastor Wendell Jones. He printed it out and gave it to me a few years ago, and believe it or not, I haven't taken it out of my wallet yet. I pull it out for inspiration as well as share it with my clients and youth I coach and mentor. It's written towards men, but it applies to women as well. I hope it serves you as it has served me.

If you keep your head when all about you

Are losing theirs and blaming it on you;

If you can trust yourself when all men doubt you,

But make allowance for their doubting too.

If you can wait and not be tired by waiting,

Or, being lied about, don't deal in lies,

Or being hated don't give way to hating,

And yet don't look to good, nor talk too wise;

If you can dream-and not make dreams your master;

If you can think-and make thoughts your aim,

If you can meet with Triumph and disaster

And treat those two imposters just the same.

If you can bear to hear the truth you've spoken

## PROCESS YOU to SUCCESS

Twisted by knaves to make a trap for fools,
Or watch the things you gave your life to, broken,
And stoop and build'em up with worn out tools;

If you can make one heap of all your winnings
And risk it on one turn of pitch-and-toss,
And lose, and start again at your beginnings,
And never breathe a word about your loss.
If you can force your heart and nerve sinew
To serve you long after they are gone,
And so hold on when there is nothing in you
Except the Will which says "Hold on!"

If you can talk with crowds and keep your virtue,
Or walk with kings –nor lose the common touch,
If neither foes nor loving friends can hurt you,
If all men count with you, but none too much,
If you can fill the unforgiving minute
With sixty seconds' worth of distance run,
Yours is the Earth and everything that's in it,
And-which is more-you'll be a Man, my son!

# Pain and Relationships

If you haven't noticed yet, my Pastor has had a major hand in my development. He once did a series on "Pain." I took plenty of notes and made personal highlights and had many personal reflections that I would like to share. It's ok to tell God your pain all while giving Him thanks. If pain isn't dealt with, it becomes depression. It has the ability to weaken your immune system and is the 4th leading cause of disease. Depression is the #1 cause "Dis-Ability": The ability to perform. Depression leads to suicide. Pain is real, but it doesn't have to be an enemy. Pain is an indication that something is out of order. When pain shows up, we should take the inner journey for answers. What's out of order? Where have I steered away from my vision or values at? If we don't address the pain in one area of our lives, it will spread into other areas. Pain cannot be quarantined, it spills over. When you leave pain un-dealt with, you end up hurting others. You will guard tender spots, all while needed others to come close.

3 reasons we miss the lessons of pain:
1. We focus on our external circumstances
2. We allow fear to rule us
3. We are forgetful people of what we have came through in past situations.

- Emotional pain says, "I am something wrong in our relationships incorrectly."
- Mental pain says, "I am something in my life incorrectly and it's causing confusion."

Pain comes with a lesson that says something is out of order. You can do anything if someone would just show you. Discover yourself. Allow yourself to go through the process of knowing yourself, choosing yourself, and giving yourself. Pain is more than just a feeling or an emotion. Pain sends the "feeling" just to get your attention, so you can listen to the message –to fix it. Don't focus on the circumstances. Don't focus on the fears. Pull out your journal an remind yourself of the past hellish situations that you have came and made it through. Pain just alerts us that we missed the lesson somewhere. We all have felt at some point that we have been done injustly. But without injustice, there would be no appreciation for true love. Injustice sets the stage for unconditional love. Lead with love. Love will give you more advantages than disadvantages. Pain is part of your path of truly becoming your true self. Pain teaches you how to truly love, and the first recipient of that love is you.

Love people you can't trust. Yes, I know it sounds crazy, but try it. Be committed to their personal development, even if that means you adding restrictions to the nature of your relationship. Trusting someone 100% says that they are predictable and that you expect them to stay the same forever. Loves says that, "I want you to grow." It's all about perspective. When you get through the pain, and stop giving in to people's tantrums, then it causes them to grow up. This is truly demonstrating emotional fitness at its finest. When you limit yourself around people because of past pain felt or experienced, you make your world smaller. You can be present, but your mind and your emotions are stuck in your past. You don't have to stay in the pain of anything, all doors of freedom are unlocked. Believe that!

To feel rejected you have to feel a loss in:

• Time

Time is a precious, depleting commodity that when given, shows others how we value them, and how we value their time.

- Intimacy
Intimacy says that we want people into our minds and heart so that we can let them know our ideas, thoughts, and dreams.

- Conversation
Conversation and communication is the only means that we have to relate. It lets other know you care. Precedence does not.

- Opportunity
Opportunity let's others bring their intellect to the table. Others need to establish a place of importance: A safe place to grow to slowly shed emotional weight.

Look at every strained relationship in your life now or every failed relationship of the past and I bet that if you search deep enough, you will be able to stress the frustration or failure to there being a lack of 1 or all of these factors from one, or both, parties. We have to be transparent from the beginning in relationships, and most importantly, learn to love ourselves first! That's why becoming emotionally fit is so important. It teaches us how to be socially responsible with others. We are our limits! We can't love others more than we love ourselves. Go into relationships being your authentic self and give others the choice to join you on your journey or not. Go into relationships "offering" acceptance, not "looking" for acceptance. It makes a difference. Give more authentic love. Get more authentic love.

Find peace within yourself and become who you were destined to be. Then, let your real crowd show up!

# Expressing Emotional Pain in a Healthy Way

Expressing Emotional Pain in a Healthy way has to first start with an accurate Self-Assessment of one's emotions, then becoming and staying self-aware of those emotions. Emotional "Self-Awareness" is noticing and being able to label your feelings, emotions, "gut-level" instincts or reactions; being able to connect these to their source; recognizing their effects on your mind and your body; using your feelings as a valuable source of insight and information about yourself, others and the situations around you. The more adept we are at discerning the force that is shaping our moods and mental status, the greater our ability to manage our behavior. We are able to choose a more constructive response -- in the moment -- based on possibilities instead of reacting to the moment based on habit. In other words, you respond with intelligence instead of impulse. The goal is to give you the tools to respond rather than simply react. The result is greater effectiveness, productivity and confidence. And, as you come to comprehend your own emotions and behavior, you increase your understanding for what drives the actions of those around you. With this knowledge, you can improve your relationships, and above all, your happiness. Social and emotional intelligence is a key factor to enhancing the quality of our lives. Below are some great tips to becoming more Emotionally Fit and "self-aware."

## Steps

For the next week, carry a watch or travel alarm with you, or set your cell phone or computer clock alarm to ring at several intervals throughout the day.

- At the times listed on the schedule, fill in the blanks with

- What you are doing, and who you are doing it with (working alone, talking with family, attending a meeting, leading a meeting, driving, eating with a friend, watching a movie alone, etc.),

- The emotion(s) you are feeling in the moment, and

- What your body is sensing at the moment, or what effect the emotion is having on your body.

Remember, you are seeking to understand your feelings. You are not trying to change them with this exercise. They are not right or wrong. Therefore, honesty is important. However, recognition alone can often diffuse or increase an emotional reaction.

- You may find that over time, the intensity of some moods decrease, while other sensations, hopefully the more pleasant ones, increase. That's why emotional intelligence helps in all aspects of your personal growth.

Regularly check in on your feelings. During the course of the day, schedule brief but frequent check–ins on your emotional state as well as what your body might be feeling or trying to tell you

# Have Something to P.R.O.V.E.

"Every morning in Africa, a gazelle wakes up. It knows it must outrun the fastest lion or it will be killed. Every morning in Africa, a lion wakes up. It knows it must run faster than the slowest gazelle, or it will starve. It doesn't matter whether you're a lion or gazelle. When the sun comes up, you'd better be running.

Lights, camera, action!!! The alarm clock goes off—do you hit the floor running or do you press snooze every day!

What do you do when the sun comes up?

What moves you?

What pushes you?

What makes you say "I can't lie here any longer?"

What do you want to prove?

**P**. passion

**R**. risk

**O**. order

136

**V.** vision

**E.** expectancy

**Passion**-the internal fire that powerfully pushes you!

**Risk**-Tight rope living that makes you go out on a limb, besides that' where the fruit is!

**Order**-Internal traffic control headquarters!

**Vision**-Whatever thou seeth, thou beeth!

**Expectancy**-living with a positive pregnant hope of things to come!

# Don't Quit

When things go wrong as they sometimes will,
When the road you're trudging seems all uphill
When the funds are low and the debts are high,
And you want to smile, but you have to sigh,
When care is pressing you down a bit—
Rest if you must, but don't quit.

Life is strange with its twists and turns,
As every one of us sometimes learns,
And many a fellow turns about
When he might have won had he stuck it out.
Don't give up though the pace seems slow—
You may succeed with another blow.

Often the goal is nearer than
It seems to a fair and faltering man,
Often the struggler has given up
When he might have captured the victor's cup,
And he learned too late when night came down,
How close he was to the golden crown.

## PROCESS YOU to SUCCESS

Success is failure turned inside out—
The silver tint of the clouds of doubt,
And you never can tell how close you are,
It may be near when it seems afar,
So stick to the fight when you're hardest hit,--
It' when things seem worst that you mustn't quit
--Author Unknown

# Tip for Emotional & Mental Detoxing

A tip from another one of my mentors from afar, Darren Hardy:

- The great <u>danger</u> of the media is that it gives us a very perverted view of the world.

- Because the focus and the repetition of messaging is on the negative, that's what our minds start believing.

- This warped and <u>narrow</u> view of what's not working has a severe <u>influence</u> on your creative potential

- It can be crippling.

- Take <u>back</u> control of your mind.


Action for today:

- Hit the <u>OFF</u> button if the source is NOT feeding your life with positive value.

- Turn off your TV if it's not feeding you positive messages.

- Turn off your radio if the lyrics are negative.

- Cancel your newspaper subscription.


*Trust me on this one.*

The   peace   and   silence   will   give   you   the   mental,   emotional, psychological and time space you need to focus on the goals and dreams you desire.

Spend less time following the news reports about other people's lives and more time leading your own.

Go make your own news today!

# End Notes

-"The 17 Essential Qualities of A Team Player"

-"Awaken the Giant Within" by Anthony Robbins

-"Becoming Emotionally Whole" by Charles Stanley

-"How to be a R.E.A.L. Success" by John Maxwell

-"If" by Rudyard Kipling

-"The Purpose of Pain Series" By Pastor Wendell Jones

-"Divorce Recovery" By Minister Angela Lipscomb

-"Success" Magazine published by Darren Hardy

-"Change Map" By 6Seconds.org

# More from the SELF Initiative

To learn of more books, products, and programs for emotional fitness, mental toughness, or social responsibility from The SELF Initiative by Jemiah Battle, please visit

www.TheSELFinitiative.com.

To book Jemiah Battle for a Keynote, Workshop, or Presentation on "Process YOU to Success: Bridging The Gap between Who You Are and Who You can Be! " please submit your request at:

Info@TheSELFinitiative.com

# Book Description

No matter your current goals, you're not going to improve your body, your career, your relationships, or your organization without first strengthening your mind! Your thoughts ultimately control your actions, and it's a strong mind that pushes us to eat right, train hard, develop & sustain healthy relationships, stay motivated, and stick to a plan for the long haul. As said by Justin Woltering, pro-performance trainer, that "even the greatest routines for nutrition, training, and supplementation will fail if you don't have the will to carry them out." We spend so much of our life people pleasing and spending tons on our outer appearance, that we often neglect our inner self. This makes us emotionally obese, socially unhealthy, and unable to handle life's most challenging problems.

In Process YOU to Success, Jemiah Battle helps you become emotionally fit and mentally tough for the game of life! He helps you understand that your success and happiness in life is a *process* not a *project*! Process YOU equips you with the tools to tackle any *obstacle* in life and truly *breakthrough* any situation! People who are emotionally fit are in control of their emotions and their behavior. They are able to handle life's challenges, build strong relationships, and recover from setbacks. But just as it requires effort to build or maintain physical health, so it is with emotional health & fitness. Information isn't enough. You have to practice!

Are you ready to become healthy and go to the next level of success, inside and out? Then let's begin the Process......

PROCESS YOU to SUCCESS

# ABOUT THE AUTHOR

Jemiah Battle, aka Mr. EQ, is founder of The SELF Initiative, an Emotional fitness trainer, and certified life coach specializing in EQ, relationship dynamics, leadership development, and social & life transitions. This book is based on the tested, results-focused strategies that he uses daily with private clients and in his own life and relationships. He believes in real world Solutions for real world people. To learn more about him and his initiatives visit

WWW.JemiahBattle.com

# CASE STUDIES for Social & Emotional Learning and Fitness (S.E.L.F. Fit™)

# The Business Case for Social + Emotional Fitness

### EQ and IQ – Just the Facts

Research indicates that one's emotional intelligence (EQ) predicts success on the job, and in life, far better than cognitive intelligence (IQ). Emotional intelligence describes the ability, capacity, or skill **to identify, assess, and manage the emotions of one's self, of others, and of groups**.
Emotionally-intelligent individuals have the ability to "tune-in" to their emotions and use this information to make better decisions and to interact more effectively with others. One's emotional intelligence is measured by their Emotional Quotient (EQ) while one's cognitive intelligence is measured by their Intelligence Quotient (IQ).

**Some estimate that our success in work and life are 90% from EQ and 10% from IQ**
**Why Emotional Intelligence Assessments are Beneficial in any Organization**

Organizations who want to be effective in today's world need an emotionally intelligent team. Becoming aware of and competent at understanding our emotions and those of others in a professional setting can guide our business thoughts and actions more positively.

**Research by Stanford University showed that 90% of those who failed as leaders**

did so because they lacked the interpersonal skills that are a critical component of emotional intelligence.

A great deal of solid, scientific research over the past few years has proven the benefits of bringing social and emotional intelligence into the workplace (or into your own personal development plans) The return on investment (ROI) for S+EI programs has been proven again and again in multiple organizations. For example:

▪ **Sanofi-Aventis Pharmaceuticals** introduced S+EI training into a development group, and had a control group which did not receive the training. They wanted to determine whether the S+EI training was cost-effective. The development group which received the training increased their S+EI scores 18% over the control group. But more importantly, the development group that received the training **outsold the control group by an average of 12%** -- or $55,200 per person per month. Multiplied by the 40 sales reps in the development group, the increase in sales was **$2,208,000 per MONTH better than the control group, for an ROI of 600%.**

▪ At **Pepsi**, S+EI programs generated a 10% increase in productivity, an 87% decrease in executive turnover **(saving $4 million), and had over a 1000% ROI**.

▪ **MetLife's** S+EI programs with selected groups resulted in S+EI trained and coached sales people **outselling their control group counterparts by 37%**.

▪ At **L'Oreal**, S+EI programs brought in $2.5 million more in sales in the first year.

▪ At **Sheraton**, S+EI programs helped **increase market share by 24%**.

▪ The reasons for losing customers and clients are 70% related to a lack of social and emotional intelligence. (The Forum Corporation on Manufacturing and Service Companies, 2004)

▪ Even the U.S. Military has embraced S+EI training, coaching, recruiting and hiring. The **U.S. Air Force** reduced turnover among military recruiters from 50% to just 4% in one year, saving the federal government over $3 million in the first year of the program.

Following is just a partial view of organizations which have benefited from S+EI programs:

PROCESS YOU to SUCCESS

The benefits listed above for organizations are both scientifically-founded and striking.

Individual benefits are even more stunning. Research indicates the following statistics for leaders, executives, managers, supervisors (and other individuals):

- 80-90% of the competencies that differentiate top performance are in the domain of emotional intelligence (Daniel Goleman, *Working with Emotional Intelligence*, 1998)

- EI is more than twice as predictive of business performance than purely cognitive intelligence (Gerald Mount in, *The Role of Emotional Intelligence in Developing International Business Capability*, 2006)

- Leaders with higher S+EI produce more powerful business results and greater profitability (Steven Stein in *Emotional Intelligence of Leaders: A Profile of Top Executives, Leadership & Organization Development Journal*, 2009).

- Turnover at the top of organizations has been accelerating in recent years, and the top career derailers are related to a lack of social and emotional intelligence (Center for Creative Leadership, 2005; Stanford University, 2001)

In fact, the 2005 study by the Center for Creative Leadership found the following issues are the **top reasons for executive derailment:**

- Poor interpersonal relationships

- Single most common factor: **being too harshly critical**

- Insensitive and/or demanding

- Alienating co-workers and direct reports

152

- Rigidity

- Inability to accept feedback about traits they need to change or improve
- Inability to listen, learn and change

- Inability to work with others

- Being disrespectful (demeaning, condescending, belittling, bullying, humiliating others)

- Being uncooperative

- Not sharing information, plans or credit

"In my experience emotional intelligence is actually more important [than book smarts] in making a leader." (Jack Welch, past CEO of GE, author, master of the turn-around)

"In the fields I have studied, emotional intelligence is much more powerful than IQ in determining who emerges as a leader. IQ is a threshold competence. You need it, but it doesn't make you a star. Emotional Intelligence can." (Warren Bennis, Researcher, Thought Leader and Author of the international bestselling book, *Becoming A Leader*)

And the **health benefits** for enhancing our personal social and emotional intelligence are even more compelling. People with high social and emotional intelligence are:

- Healthier

- Experience lower rates of chronic illness

• Have lower disease risks

• Have fewer symptoms and less pain when they do fall ill

• Less likely to have high blood pressure, heart attacks, diabetes, or a stroke

• More likely to live longer, up to ten years longer!

(Cohen, S. & Doherty, R., *Psychological Bulletin*, 2005, and Fredrickson, B., *Positivity*, 2009)

Research also shows the following outcomes of healthy, positive emotions:

- Improved performance and achievement

- Greater creativity and innovative problem-solving

- Better decision-making

- More flexible thought processes

- Improved memory

- Improved hormonal balance

Amazingly, research has also shown that:

- **People with positive emotions earn more over the course of their lifetimes.** (Diener, E., *Social Indicators Research*, 2002)

▪ **People with positive emotions have more satisfying marriages.**
(Harker, L. & Keltner, D., *Journal of Personality and*
*Social Psychology*, 2001)


*Servant-Leadership Development & Emotional Fitness starts*
*with Awareness...*

# A Case for Social & Emotional Intelligence in Our School Systems By The Emotional Intelligence Network presented by Jemiah Battle, CPCC

## Executive Summary

Emotional intelligence (EQ) is the ability to use emotions effectively and productively. Since the publication of the initial research in 1990, innovative schools and educational organizations have begun integrating emotional intelligence into their educational programs. It is becoming increasingly clear that these skills are one of the foundations for high-performing students and classrooms.

When emotional intelligence began to attract the public attention, there were few model programs. In his 1995 book, *Emotional Intelligence*, Daniel Goleman described two of the preeminent programs, a class in some New Haven schools, and the *Self-Science* curriculum.1 As the benefits of emotional intelligence have become more widely recognized and investigated, several implementation strategies have been designed. These include assessments, training programs, and educational curricula that assist educators to build emotional intelligence. Current research in education, psychology, and related fields is accumulating to show the benefits of Social Emotional Learning (SEL) programs for children as young as preschoolers. Public awareness is catching up to the research. Recently a *New York Times* editorial reviewed key research findings and concluded,

157

PROCESS YOU to SUCCESS

**"…social and emotional learning programs significantly improve students' academic performance."**2 Additional research also shows emotional intelligence is strongly linked to staying in school, avoiding risk behaviors, and improving health, happiness, and life success. Several organizations have emerged to help schools and organizations implement emotional intelligence and social-emotional learning programs, including The Collaborative for Academic, Social and Emotional Learning (CASEL), The George Lucas Educational Foundation (GLEF), The Center for Social Emotional Learning, CSEE, and Six Seconds, The Emotional Intelligence Network.

# Introduction

Emotional intelligence (EQ)3 is emerging as a critical factor for sustaining high achievement, retention, a positive behavior as well as improving life success. Increasingly, schools and educational organizations are turning to EQ seeking a systemic solution to improve outcomes – both academic and social (such as school attrition, student satisfaction, peer relationships, and health).

What's driving this interest? Is emotional intelligence "just a fad," or does the science offer new insight and tools that genuinely affect performance? And if EQ is so important, how do educators find their way to the value amidst the hype? *American Psychologist*, one of the most prestigious sources of peer reviewed psychological research, has released several articles on emotional intelligence. In particular, these reports have demonstrated time-tested support for school-based emotional intelligence prevention and intervention programs leading researchers to conclude: "There is a solid and growing empirical base concluding that well-designed, well-implemented school-based prevention and youth development programming can positively influence a diverse array of social, health, and academic outcomes."4 In a time of budget cuts, intense societal pressures on youth, and national testing standards, the strain on educational funds to fulfill the diverse needs of our children is becoming increasingly apparent. This calls for innovative approaches to addressing the academic, social, psychological, and physical health needs of developing students. Because of its wide ranging impact, emotional intelligence prevention and intervention programming may be the key investment that secures a positive future for our children.

## What is Emotional Intelligence?

*Emotional intelligence is the ability to perceive emotions, to access and*

160

*generate emotions so as to assist thought, to understand emotions and emotional knowledge, and to reflectively regulate emotions so as to promote emotional and intellectual growth.*– Mayer & Salovey, 1997.5

Most people first heard the term "emotional intelligence" around 1995 with the publication of Daniel Goleman's best-selling book *Emotional Intelligence.* In that work, Goleman laid out a powerful case that such factors as self-awareness, self-discipline, and empathy determine personal and professional success. He drew on the work of numerous leading scientists and authors who were working to define and measure the skills of emotional intelligence.6 Drawing on Goleman's definition and incorporating the original research by top scientists in the field, Six Seconds set out to create a definition of how to put emotional intelligence into action. Therefore their definition is simple and direct: Emotional intelligence is the capacity to blend thinking and feeling to make optimal decisions.

Researchers once said emotions impede thinking, but in the last decades they've found that emotions actually are critical to thinking. EQ researchers are identifying:

# What is EQ?

Some people just know how to get along with others; some people are more self-confident, and some are great at inspiring people. All these require people to be smart about feelings. Emotional intelligence can be applied through a set of learnable skills that include identifying and changing emotions, motivating yourself, and empathizing with another person. Almost anyone can learn the EQ skills to build more successful relationships. For children, EQ helps increase academic success, bolster stronger friendships, and reduce risk behaviors. For adults, EQ skills are critical for career .

- The way emotions and thinking interact to create our awareness and decision-making..
- How emotions are essential to successful human interaction.
- What processes are involved in learning to use and manage emotions more effectively.

The research is beginning to demonstrate what many educators, counselors, parents, and other observers had long recognized – that the most successful people were not necessarily those with high IQs but rather those with highly developed interpersonal and social skills. Today many prominent psychologists and researchers agree EQ is an intelligence that is separate from cognitive intelligence (IQ) and has components that are different from traditional measures of personality. There were several pioneers who have helped raise this awareness. Peter Salovey is a dean and professor of psychology at Yale University. Jack Mayer is a professor at the University of New Hampshire. The two psychologists published the first academic

definition of emotional intelligence in 1990, and have continued as
the leading
researchers in the field. Reuven BarOn, a psychologist and researcher
at University of Texas Medical Branch, is another pioneer in the field.
He created the first validated measure of "emotionally intelligent
behavior," the EQ-i.7 Other leading in this area include Joseph
LeDoux, Antonio Damasio, and educators such as Karen McCown,
Anabel Jensen, and Maurice Elias. Now there are several statistically
reliable measures of emotional intelligence and emotional
competence for adults and two measures for children.

These assessments are being used to demonstrate the links between emotional intelligence and performance. One of the newest tools is called the "Six Seconds Emotional Intelligence Assessment-Youth Version," or "SEI-YV."8 The SEI-YV is unique because it provides a link between EQ skills and life outcomes (such as academic achievement and health). Moreover it offers an actionable model to improve. One of the important components of emotional intelligence is the accurate appraisal of emotion. Identifying and naming emotions is generally identified as "Emotional Literacy," which is a competence central to many social-emotional learning programs. Recent research on emotional literacy demonstrates the bridge between cognition (analytical thinking, such as use of language), affect (experience of emotion), and physiology (the body's response). A team at UCLA used fMRI (functional magnetic resonance imaging, a tool that shows very specific brain activity) to assess how emotion is regulated. In the study, 30 adults, ages 18-36, where given different mechanisms for processing emotional datum. It turns out that naming emotions reduces the emotional reaction (in the amygdala, the part of the brain responsible for fight-flight-freeze reactions). 9 In other words, when thoughts and feelings are working together – when emotional intelligence is working – people are able to self-regulate their feelings and reduce the kind of reactivity that otherwise escalates.

In addition to assessing individual emotional intelligence, it is possible to ascertain the emotional context, or climate, of a school or organization. While not strictly a measure of emotional intelligence *per se*, it makes sense that if people in the group are effectively using their emotional intelligence to manage behavior, perceptions of the climate will be generally more positive. Emotional intelligence is not, in itself, sufficient to create optimal outcomes for youth. However, the way emotional intelligence is used, both by youth and those who support them has a powerful effect on the children's lives, yet it is frequently ignored. Emotional intelligence appears to be a core ingredient that, when developed and well employed, has wide-ranging benefits for learning, relationships, and wellness. Everyone has emotional intelligence. For most of us, it's an underdeveloped area and an untapped resource. Peter Salovey said, "Yes we can control emotions. The trick is doing it in the right way at the right time."10 This concept has a long history; around 350 BC, Aristotle wrote, "Anyone can become angry -- that is easy. But to be angry with the right person, to the right degree, at the right time, for the right purpose, and in the right way, that is not easy." The research progress in the last 15 years is remarkable; it's becoming increasing clear how emotion and cognition function together, and how we perceive and process emotional information. At the same time, other intelligence research has been underway for over 100 years, so emotional intelligence remains an emerging science.

Meanwhile, worldwide, thousands of schools, counselors, and educators, and millions of parents, are utilizing the new findings to help young people thrive.

# EQ and Academic Achievement

The introduction of emotional intelligence and social emotional learning curricula has sparked a new field of research examining the efficacy of EQ intervention programs. So far, the results indicate that emotional intelligence has extraordinary potential as a mediator of positive school outcomes.

For example, in a 2004 study of 667 high school students, James Parker and team gave students an
emotional intelligence assessment and compared those scores to their year-end grades.

EQ and academic performance are strongly related. 11 Participants in a study were asked to complete an EQ inventory between the first and second semesters of the academic year. At the end of the year, each EQ response was matched with the student's final grade point average. Students were then divided into three groups based on their grade point percentiles: highest achievement (80th percentile and above); lowest achievement (20th percentile and below); middle (between the 80th and 20th grade point percentiles). The following results were observed:

- Students in the highest achievement group also demonstrated greater interpersonal competency, adaptability, and stress management than students in the other groups.
- Students in the middle percentile group scored significantly higher than the 20th percentile group for interpersonal competency, adaptability, and stress management.

In a study of the *Self-Science* SEL curriculum including 311 students in 13 classrooms, teachers identified the program to be highly effective in improving both classroom relationships and academic performance. In their meta-analysis of 379 SEL prevention and youth development interventions, Durlak & Weissberg reported that SEL intervention programs produced a variety of positive student outcomes including achievement (see box to lower right).13 Perhaps one reason these studies are showing such large effects is that SEL Programs Proven to Improve

- Personal and social competencies
- Decreased antisocial behavior and aggression
- Fewer serious discipline problems and school suspensions
- Increased acceptance among peers
- Better school attendance
- Higher grade point averages
- Higher academic achievement scores13

"…Social and emotional learning students have significantly better attendance records; their classroom behavior is more constructive and less often disruptive; they like school more; and they have better grade point averages. They are also less likely to be suspended or otherwise disciplined."2 Timothy Shriver & Roger Weissberg, *The New York Times 12*

100% of the teachers reported that Self- Science increases cooperation and improves classroom relationships. In addition, they agreed (92%) that the program helped:

- Increase student focus/attention
- Improve teacher/student relationships

The teachers also agreed (77-85%) that it worked to:

- Improve student learning
- Enhance collaborative work
- Increase positive verbal statements
- Decrease "put downs" (negative verbal messages) between students12; Students are under a great deal of stress, which can easily derail them.

Applying emotional intelligence skills appears to be an effective coping mechanism. For example, Petrides, Frederickson, and Furnham suggest that specific aspects of emotional intelligence may be especially important for students at risk. Specifically, their research suggests that students who struggle academically face even greater pressures than their peers. High EQ may serve to mediate, and thus dampen, the effects of associated stressors making all the difference between acceptable and unacceptable academic performance.14 In parallel to an individual student's capacity to cope, the school environment likewise has a major affect on performance. When students feel a sense of belonging in a respectful environment, they are more free to focus on their academic work. One of the ways SEL programs seem to improve academic achievement is by improving the school climate. Focusing attention on feelings and helping students and adults recognize the emotional impact of their choices may foster a more positive climate. The Assessment of School Climate examines four aspects of the school climate: Empathy (feeling cared for), Accountability (sense of follow-through), Respect (considerate behavior), and Trust (belief in the people and institution). These factors are highly predictive of three critical outcomes: Connectedness, Learning, and Safety. These outcomes are combined into a "School Performance" variable.

In summary, emotional intelligence is strongly linked to academic performance. High EQ seems to help youth manage the complexities and pressures that would otherwise derail them. This effect occurs both on an individual basis and in terms of the overall school climate. Among other noted benefits of emotional intelligence, studies suggest that students with higher emotional intelligence tend to demonstrate better school attendance than their classmates with lower EQ scores. Given the importance of staying in school both for academic and life success, the link between EQ and retention will be examined next.

## EQ and Academic Retention

According to the United States Department of Education's Office of Educational Research and Improvement, 5% of high school sophomores, juniors, and seniors dropped out of high school in the 1999 school year (a rate that is consistent since the late 1980's). Furthermore, in 2000, nearly 11% of the 3.8 million 16- to 24-year olds in the US failed to earn a high school diploma.16  Rumberger suggests that the personal consequences of dropping out of high school may include decreased economic benefit as a result of insufficient academic skill, as well as poorer psychological and physical health that arises as an indirect result of from employment and income challenges.17 The fact is school attrition hurts our students and our communities (please see NCSET18).

Recent studies of EQ and college retention indicate that students with higher emotional intelligence are less likely to drop out of school than their peers. Parker, Hogan, Eastabrook, Oke and Wood matched a sample of 213 individuals who had dropped out of their universities before the beginning of their second year with a group of 213 individuals who stayed with their academic programs. After accounting for age, gender, and ethnicity, results of the study suggested that the persistent group had significantly higher levels of EQ, interpersonal competency, adaptability, and stress management than students who withdrew from their programs.It appears that emotional intelligence is an important indicator of students staying in school.

# EQ and Prevention

In addition to academic success and school retention, many studies have examined the relationship between emotional intelligence, health, and behavior. In his 1995 book, *Emotional Intelligence*, Daniel Goleman wrote about two model social emotional learning (SEL) programs; one is called Self- Science. Goleman asserted that EQ education is a critical component for improving life-outcomes: "Self-Science is an almost point-for-point match with the ingredients of emotional intelligence – and with the core skills recommended as primary prevention for the range of pitfalls threatening children."[20] Studies now document this link, showing how developing emotional competence reduces risky behaviors (such as drug use, dropping out, and violence) while increasing pro-social behaviors (such as exercise, positive peer relationships, and leadership). As mentioned above, the Self-Science[12] and Durlak & Weissberg[13] studies found SEL programs improved student behavior. Likewise the retention data indicates high emotional intelligence may help youth mitigate stressors that could lead them to leave school – perhaps this same capacity helps people avoid other risky behaviors. The pro-social benefits of emotional intelligence begin at a very young age. In a study of four-year-olds, 51 preschoolers were observed, tracking how they behaved and how they were accepted by peers. Then they were *Youth EQ scores are strongly correlated with scores on important life outcomes (a composite of health, relationships, satisfaction, achievement, and efficacy).*[24] tested to see how much knowledge they had about emotions. Those with higher emotion knowledge were less involved in aggressive interactions and more accepted by their peers.[21] This trend continues in elementary school. In a study of 160 students (mean age 10.8), those with higher EQ scores were recognized by teachers and peers both as cooperative and as leaders, and for being neither disruptive nor aggressive.[22] By middle school, the challenges become more severe, with middle schoolers experimenting with many risky behaviors including using alcohol or tobacco. Dennis Trinidad and Anderson Johnson assessed 205 middle school students in southern California, measuring both emotional intelligence and use of alcohol and tobacco. The teens with higher emotional intelligence were less likely to use alcohol and tobacco.[23] In one of the largest studies to date, Carina Fiedeldey-van Dijk and the Six Seconds' team assessed an international sample of 2,665 youth ages 7-18.

The study compared scores on the Six Seconds Emotional Intelligence Assessment – Youth Version with a composite "Barometer of Life" comprised of Good Health, Relationship Quality, Life Satisfaction, Personal Achievement, and Self-Efficacy. As shown in the graph, EQ scores are strongly correlated with these outcomes.24

# How Huge Could This Be For Global Education As We

# Know It?

In a fascinating study of teenage behavior, Mayer, Perkins, Caruso, and Salovey tested adolescents for EI and verbal IQ.25 The teens were asked *"Think about the last time you were out with some friends and they wanted to do something you were uncomfortable with (e.g., it seemed risky or not a good choice)."* The responses illustrate that increased emotional intelligence helps teenagers make more complex, sophisticated, and pro-social decisions. There are several EQ studies with college students that reinforce the data presented above. Marc Brackett and team have conducted studies on self-care, academics, personal relationships, and behavior. In one study they found significant correlations between low EI and negative behaviors (e.g., use of drugs and alcohol, violence, vandalism), especially for males.26

For example, a study of 365 students and adults in Greece (mean age 25) found a strong correlation between EQ and issues with anxiety and with overall health.27

Six Seconds' researchers had 665 adults complete the SEI assessment28 and a questionnaire about success factors. The success factor questionnaire included items about health, quality of life, effectiveness, and– outcomes combined into a Life Success variable. Regression analysis revealed a strong relationship: 54.79% of variation in Life Success is explained by scores on the SEI.29

# Related Research

With mounting evidence that EQ and SEL programs improve school outcomes, several additional
questions arise, including:

- Can student EQ improve?
- Can parent EQ improve?
- How does EQ help educators?

To address student improvement, Six Seconds conducted a study of 13 different classrooms for six weeks; prior to the start, students completed an assessment, then had six lessons, then another assessment. While the data suggests that EQ training would be most effective with a longer period of training, results show that students' EQ increased significantly with even relatively brief exposure to the program. One class of 26 seventh graders increased by almost 5 points on the EQi-YV.30 This finding led Reuven Bar-On (the creator of the EQi assessment) to write: "At the end of the first year, the children were better able to understand and express themselves, to understand and relate with others, to manage and control their emotions, and to adapt to their immediate school environment. These important changes suggest that this program is viable."31 To understand how parents could be taught EQ skills, and how these skills would then affect their children, Sue McNamara conducted a study in which she administered an interview and the SEI assessment, then delivered four weeks of parent education using the "EQ for Families" program,32 and then followed-up with a post-interview and a repeat of the SEI assessment. Parents also kept a daily journal. Parents' scores increased significantly and according to their journals and exit interviews, family interactions became much more positive.33

*This study found that scores went up significantly after four workshops teaching parents emotional intelligence skills.*33

In addition to the benefits to children and parents, developing emotional intelligence helps educators. For example, Stone, Parker, and Wood studied 464 principals and vice-principals in Ontario. They concluded that overall EQ was a significant predictor of administrative success.34 That is, educators with high EQ were more often rated as above average administrators by both supervisors and staff. As shown in the graph below, the administrators who were rated "above average" also had a significantly higher level of EQ.

*School administrators rated above average also have higher levels of EQ — indicating emotional intelligence is connected with leadership performance.34*

# Conclusion

In an era when children frequently feel disconnected from friends and family, where rapid social change is the norm, when media and sports stars demonstrate poor behavior,35 educators recognize the human need for developing social and emotional skills. At the same time, school budgets are being cut while pressure is being intensified to improve test scores – leaving many educators with a perceived dichotomy. They believe the choice is either nurture children or help them achieve. Fortunately, the compelling evidence shows that it is not an either/or choice; rather, the data says addressing children's social and emotional needs is an effective way to improve academic achievement. Research has illustrated how EQ can substantially decrease anti-social behavior and aggression, school suspensions, and discipline problems while increasing personal and social competency, school attendance, satisfaction, and academic achievement.36 This overwhelming body of new findings has led to a powerful conclusion: "direct intervention in the psychological determinants of learning promise the most effective avenues of reform."37 Social and emotional development is central to children's success in school. By incorporating EQ into existing educational programs, we can promote our children's achievement in the present and secure their success for the future.

## End Notes

Technical Note: There are many different models and definitions of emotional intelligence – this is normal for a new scientific discipline. Even the field of "classical intelligence" has not achieved a unified definition of IQ after over 100 years (hence the many different IQ tests available). This paper uses examples from many models, primarily the Mayer-Salovey-Caruso model measured by the MSCEIT, the Bar-On model measured by the EQi, and the Six Seconds model measured by the SEI.

1 Goleman, D (1995) *Emotional Intelligence: Why it can matter more than IQ*. New York: Bantam.

2 Shriver, T.P., & Weissberg, R.P. (2005, August 16). "No emotion left behind," *The New York Times*.

3 "EQ" is an abbreviation for "Emotional Quotient," and is used in this document with emotional intelligence.

4 Greenbert, M.T., Weissberg, R.P., O'Brien, M.U., Zins J.E., Fredericks, L., Resnick, H., & Elias, M.J. (2003). "Enhancing school-based prevention and youth development through coordinated social, emotional, and academic learning," *American Psychologist* 58 (6/7), 466-474.

5 Mayer, J. D., & Salovey, P. (1997). "What is emotional intelligence?" In Salovey, P. & Sluyter, D. (Eds.), *Emotional development and emotional intelligence: Implications* for *educators* (pp. 3-31). New York: Basic Books.

6 Goleman, D (1995) *Emotional Intelligence: Why it can matter more than IQ*. New York: Bantam.

7 Bar-On, R. (1997). The Bar-On Emotional Quotient Inventory (EQ-i). Toronto: Multi- Health Systems.

8 Jensen, A. & Fieldeldey-van Dijk, C. (2007). *Six Seconds Emotional Intelligence Assessment – Youth Version (SEI-YV)*. San Francisco: Six Seconds.

9 Activity in the amygdala seems to be mitigated via interaction with an area of the brain that may be critical to "thinking through" self-regulation (right ventrolateral prefrontal cortex). This graph shows a

strong relationship (r=-.51) between the cortex and amydala as the subjects named emotions. Lieberman, Matthew D, Naomi I. Eisenberger, Molly J. Crockett, Sabrina M. Tom, Jennifer H. Pfeifer, Baldwin M. Way
(2007) "Putting Feelings Into Words: Affect Labeling Disrupts Amygdala Activity in
Response to Affective Stimuli" *Psychological Science*, Vol. 18, Issue 5, Page 421.
10 Salovey, P. (2003). Personal correspondence to Joshua Freedman, unpublished.
11 The EQi:YV was used, total EQ vs grades showed a Cronbach coefficient alpha of r=.41 (using a Path model). Parker, J.D.A., Creque, R.E., Barnhart, D.L., Harris, J.I., Majeski, S.A., Wood, L.M., Bond, B.J., & Hogan, M.J. (2004). "Academic achievement in high school, does emotional intelligence matter?" *Personality and Individual Differences*, 37,1321-1330.
12 Freedman, J. (2003). "Key Lessons from 35 Years of Social-Emotional Education: How Self-Science Builds Self-Awareness, Positive Relationships, and Healthy Decision-Making." *Perspectives in Education* 21(4):69-80.
13 Durlak & Weissberg, R.P. (2005) as cited in Cherniss, C., Extein, M., Goleman, D., Weissberg, R.P. (2006). "Emotional intelligence: What does the research really indicate?" *Educational Psychologist*, 41 (4), 239-245.
14 Petrides, K. V., Frederickson, N., & Furnham, A. (2004). "The role of trait emotional intelligence in academic performance and deviant behavior at school."

*Personality and Individual Differences* 36 (2004) 277–293

15 Jensen, A. & Freedman, J. (2006). *Assessment of School Climate.* San Francisco: Six Seconds. Regression analysis from Freedman, J. & Fieldeldey-van Dijk, C. "White Paper: School Climate and School Success," Six Seconds (in press).

16 Kaufman, P., Alt, M.N., Chapman, C.D. (2001). "Dropout rates in the United States, 2000." *Statistical Analysis Report.* MPR, Berkeley: CA.

17 Rumberger, R.W. (1987). "High school dropouts: A review of issues and evidence." *Review of Educational Research,* 57(2), 101-121.

18 National Center on Secondary Education and Transition. "Part 1: What do we know about dropout prevention?" Retrieved June 20, 2007 from http://www.ncset.org/publications/essentialtools/dropout/part1.1.asp

19 Parker, J.D.A., Hogan, M.J., Eastabrook, J.M., Oke, A., & Wood, L.M. (2006). "Emotional intelligence and student retention: Predicting the successful transition from high school to university." *Personality and Individual Differences,* 41, 1329- 1336.

20 Goleman, D. (1995). *Emotional Intelligence: Why it can matter more than IQ.* New York: Bantam.

21 Arsenio, W.F., Cooperman, S., & Lover, A. (2000). "Affective predictors of preschoolers' aggression and acceptance: Direct and indirect effects." *Developmental Psychology,* 36 (4), 438-448.

22 Petrides, K.V., Sangareau, Y., Furnham, A., & Frederickson, N. (2006). "Trait emotional intelligence and children's peer relations at school." *Social Development,* 15 (3),537-547.

23 Tobacco use vs EI, r2=0.11 p<.001 -- Alcohol use vs EI, r2=0.10 p<.001 -- Trinidad, D.R. & Johnson, C.A. (2002). "The association between emotional intelligence and early adolescent tobacco and alcohol use." *Personality and Individual Differences,* 32 (1), 95-105.

24 Fiedeldey-Van Dijk, C. & Jensen, A. (2007). *Six Seconds Emotional Intelligence Assessment Youth Version (SEI-YV) – Technical Manual,* Six Seconds (in press).

25 Mayer, J. D., Perkins, D., Caruso, D. R., & Salovey, P. (2001). "Emotional intelligence and giftedness." *Roeper Review,* 23, 131-137.

26 One important aspect of this study was the control for both personality and academic achievement – in other words, even with those important factors taken out, EI (based on the MSCEIT assessment) was significant. Brackett, M.A., Mayer, J.D., Warner, R.M. (2004). "Emotional Intelligence and its relation to everyday behaviour." *Personality and Individual Differences,* 36 (6), 1387-1402.

27 EQ anxiety, r=-.42, EQ and overall health problems, r= -.49, p<.01 -- Tsaousis, I. & Nikolaou, I. (2005). "Exploring the relationship of emotional intelligence with physical and psychological health functioning." *Stress and Health,* March 3, Wiley InterScience.

28 Freedman, J, Ghini, M. & Jensen, A. (2005). *Six Seconds Emotional Intelligence Assessment (SEI).* San Francisco: Six Seconds.

29 Freedman, J., Ghini, M., & Fieldeldey-van Dijk, C. (2006). "White Paper: Emotional Intelligence and Performance," www.6seconds.org/sei.

30 Total EQ increased from 54.7 to 59.8, z-value=3.61, p <.000, Freedman, J. (2003). "Key Lessons from 35 Years of Social-Emotional Education: How Self-Science Builds Self-Awareness, Positive Relationships, and Healthy Decision-Making." *Perspectives in Education* 21(4):69-80.

31 Bar-On, R. (2007). "How Important Is It to Educate People to Be Emotionally Intelligent, and Can It Be Done?" *Educating People to Be Emotionally Intelligent*, Praeger, (1) 10.

32 Freedman, J. & Jensen, A. (2005). *EQ for Families: Family Education Workshops on Emotional Intelligence*, Six Seconds.

33 McNamara, S. (2006) "Emotional Intelligence, The Generation Game: Learn the Rules so children will too!" Unpublished Masters Thesis.

34 Stone, H., Parker, J.D.A., & Wood, L.M. (2005). "Report on the Ontario Principals' Council leadership study." Toronto: Ontario Principals' Council

35 For data on these conditions, see the World Health Organization "Health and Health Behavior Among Young People," or The Monitoring the Future Survey (monitoringthefuture.org), cited in Freedman, J. (2007). "Special advice for dads" in *At the Heart of Leadership: How to Get Results with Emotional Intelligence*. San Francisco: Six Seconds.

36 Cherniss, C., Extein, M., Goleman, D., Weissberg, R.P. (2006). "Emotional intelligence: What does the research really indicate?" *Educational Psychologist*, 41(4), 239-245.

37 Wang, M.C., Haertel, G.D., & Walberg, H.J. (1997). Learning influences. In H.J. Walberg & G.D. Haertel (Eds.) *Psychology and Educational Practice* (p.199-211). Berkeley, CA: McCatchan (210).

PROCESS YOU to SUCCESS

www.ingramcontent.com/pod-product-compliance
Lightning Source LLC
Chambersburg PA
CBHW070039100426
42740CB00013B/2735